# SUBMITTED UNTO PERFECTION

# SUBMITTED UNTO PERFECTION

## Reflections for the Bride of Christ

### Jo Gwost

ELM HILL

A Division of
HarperCollins Christian Publishing

www.elmhillbooks.com

© 2018 Jo Gwost

## Submitted Unto Perfection
### Reflections for the Bride of Christ

Published in Nashville, Tennessee, by Elm Hill, an imprint of Thomas Nelson. Elm Hill and Thomas Nelson are registered trademarks of HarperCollins Christian Publishing, Inc.

Elm Hill titles may be purchased in bulk for educational, business, fund-raising, or sales promotional use. For information, please e-mail SpecialMarkets@ThomasNelson.com.

**Library of Congress Cataloging-in-Publication Data**

Library of Congress Control Number:  2018953401

ISBN 978-1-595559012 (Paperback)
ISBN 978-1-595558985 (Hardbound)
ISBN 978-1-595558909 (eBook)

# DEDICATION

*To all the people who choose
to magnify God in His perfection.*

# PREFACE

Somewhere within these pages may you find something that triggers within your heart a deeper love and devotion to God.

I pray that you experience the joy of being submitted and obedient to our great God and Father.

# CONTENTS

"Whom will he teach knowledge?
And whom will he make to understand the message?
Those just weaned from milk?
Those just drawn from the breasts?
For precept, must be upon precept, precept upon precept,
Line upon line, line upon line,
Here a little, there a little."

– ISAIAH 28.9–10

# PORTRAIT

Eternal
Ancient of Days
Abounding with Youth
God

Justice
Filled with Mercy
Washed in Love
Eyes

A mouth that drips Honey
Nourishing and Meat
Fragrance that permeates the Flesh
Righting the Soul

White and Ruddy
Overlaid with Beauty
Exquisite Within
Abounding with Mercy
Fitly King
Altogether Lovely

*My beloved is white and ruddy, Chief among ten thousand.*
*His head is like the finest gold; His locks are wavy, and black as a raven.*
*His eyes are like doves by the rivers of waters, washed with milk,*
*and fitly set. His cheeks are like a bed of spices, banks of scented herbs.*
*His lips are lilies, dripping liquid myrrh. His hands are rods of gold set*

*with beryl. His body is carved ivory inlaid with sapphires.*
*His legs are pillars of marble set on bases of fine gold.*
*His countenance is like Lebanon, excellent as the cedars.*
*His mouth is most sweet, yes, he is altogether lovely.*
*This is my beloved, and this is my friend,*
*O daughters of Jerusalem!*
– SONG OF SOLOMON 5:10–16

# STILL ME

There's not so much that needs be done
Just help me worship the Holy One
Into Your arms Father I would flee
In Your mercy come to me

Still my heart its quaking quest
Bid me come as Thy dear guest
Ever only eyes for Thee

'Til in transport I would be
At Your feet I humbly bow
Help me, Lord! Oh! Help me now!

*God is in the midst of her, she shall not be moved;*
*God shall help her, just at the break of dawn.*

*– PSALM 46:5*

# IMPRINT

Oh Lord! What's wrong with me?

You are as I have made thee.
No mistake
No retake
Just fine
You're mine.

*So God created man in His own image;*
*in the image of God He created him;*
*male and female He created them.*
*– GENESIS 1:27*

# FIRM CHOICE
## SHAKY START

Lord, I choose Your way this day in all things.
The choice is made.

Now, Father, help me to discern clearly
Your will in all situations.
Do not put me to the test, for I am
But dust and know my shifting sand.

Instead, Lord, guide my way in right paths,
And in mercy help and unfold the day.
Thank You for Your deep understanding.
Help me to see and know
The Christ of my Heart.

Amen.

*But as for me and my house, we will serve the LORD.*
*– JOSHUA 24:15*

# Stirred

Do I really *know* that Christ lives within me? I have knowledge to be sure. I've read scripture and I know what it says, but do I really believe it? How does one live a life of faith?

What does it mean to live a life of service to God? Perhaps I have been able to hammer out a life of service to other people. Being an active participant in the needs of church, home, neighborhood, school, and community can look pretty good, but does that mean service to God? It might.

We are all asked to serve and love others on behalf of Christ, especially the Body of Believers, the Church. But what is it to really know that God Himself lives within me and to serve Him? I suppose it might look the same as serving others, for that love He has for people is expressed through the good deeds of His children.

*Therefore, whether you eat or drink, or whatever you do,*
*do all to the glory of God.*
*– 1 Corinthians 10:31*

There is however, an ache in my heart to become aware that God lives within me and to tremble at that holy revelation. I desire to be aware of His holy presence, to *know* He lives in my heart. I am a holy vessel of the Holy Spirit—God in me.

*To them God willed to make known what are the riches of the*
*glory of this mystery among the Gentiles: which is Christ in you,*
*the hope of glory.*
*– Colossians 1:27*

How I want this to stir in my heart and soul until it remains front and center in my thinking! I want it to be real to me. Faith proclaims that it should be.

*That Christ may dwell in your hearts through faith.*
*– EPHESIANS 3:17A*

Jesus Himself is the one who pens faith upon my heart. In Him I can trust that this deep and holy desire as I keep it fed on His Words will become more and more a part of my life.

*That the genuineness of your faith, being much more precious*
*than gold that perishes, though it is tested by fire, may be found to*
*praise, honor, and glory at the revelation of Jesus Christ.*
*– 1 PETER 1:7*

As I submit to His perfecting hand, there is joy in the present. Although there is lack in this area, faith rises up to meet the presence of God at the throne of mercy and grace. He forgives so freely my apathy and lukewarm attitude regarding His holy presence within me. He freely multiplies the grace to help and grow me in all the places of my deepest desires for Him.

*Therefore, He is also able to save to the uttermost those who come*
*to God through Him, since He always lives to make*
*intercession for them.*
*– HEBREWS 7:25*

As I work with the Lord and His mercy and grace toward me, I sense an awakening in my heart that draws me nearer to Him. There comes a deeper longing just to be close to Him and let His light shine upon and through me. I want to spend time being alone with Him in silence, with no requests, no petitions, just there at His dear nail-scarred feet in reverent awe.

I think this would please Him.

> *And do this, knowing the time, that now it is high time*
> *to awake out of sleep; for now our salvation is nearer*
> *than when we first believed.*
> *– ROMANS 13:11*

> *Arise, shine;*
> *For your light has come!*
> *And the glory of the LORD is risen upon you.*
> *For behold, the darkness shall cover the earth,*
> *And deep darkness the people;*
> *But the LORD will arise over you,*
> *And His glory will be seen upon you.*
> *– ISAIAH 60:1–2*

# MY HOPELESSNESS HIS POWER

The hopelessness of the crucified Christ—drained of lifeblood, depleted of water, dead—puts my hopeless condition and the mightiness of God's power and mercy into deeper perspective. God brought Jesus to life when conditions were totally hopeless. No less me. I was rotting in hopeless sin. When there was nothing I could do, no price I could pay, no sweet wiles I could use or fancy talk I could make to earn or attain redemption, God reached me. God moved. God put His plan into motion to give life to me. The same Spirit of Life that raised Christ Jesus from the dead gave me victory over sin and death. His righteousness is mine. His life infuses me.

I search
Cry out
Desperate for the touch of Your
Nail-scarred hand
Longing beneath the flood of
Living Water

Your Word finds me
Stilled for a moment
My soul rests

Behold
He covers

*In Him we have redemption through His blood, the forgiveness*
*of sins, according to the riches of His grace.*
*– EPHESIANS 1:7*

# TEND WITH PATIENCE

There are little flashing glimpses coming my way lately involving the impact of what our Lord Jesus Christ did for us on the cross. Perhaps the old seeds of long-ago teachings are beginning to awaken and take root in my heart as I water it with the Word. No matter where I read in Scripture, these brief stirrings touch my mind. It makes my heart wake up in anticipation of deeper insight. Insight that calls life forth and changes me. The hunger to receive with ownership all that God has for me.

Loaf rising
Forming
Lending volume
Inhaling breath
From God
Nourishment
Bit by little bit
Who would take a bite?

*But the ones that fell on the good ground are those who, having heard the word with a noble and good heart, keep it and bear fruit with patience.*

*– LUKE 8:15*

# ENLISTED

Rule and reign
Correct and train
Let nothing hinder my growth
In becoming
Like Jesus

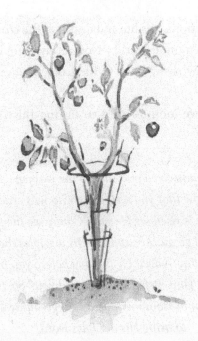

*You therefore must endure hardship as a good soldier of JesusChrist. No one engaged in warfare entangles himself with the affairs of this life, that he may please him who enlisted him as a soldier. And also, if anyone competes in athletics, he is not crowned unless he competes according to the rules.*

– 2 TIMOTHY 2:3-5

# WHAT NOW

Moses shouted to Pharaoh, "Let my people go!" God's words. And God ripped the people of Israel from the land of Egypt and Pharaoh's grasp with mighty signs and wonders. He even plundered Egypt, giving favor to His chosen people by loading them with goods freely given by the Egyptians. The Psalmist says there was not one feeble among them. Wow!

Wasn't it Jesus' actions, His life and death on the cross that shouted to Satan and all the fallen underworld, "Now let my people go!"? He punctuated His demand by rising back to life from the dead and ascending into heaven!

What then can we look forward to during this time, the close of the Age?

> But the angel answered and said to the women, "Do not be
> afraid, for I know that you seek Jesus who was crucified. He is
> not here; for He is risen, as He said. Come, see the place where
> the Lord lay. And go quickly and tell His disciples that He is risen
> from the dead, and indeed He is going before you into Galilee;
> there you will see Him. Behold, I have told you." So, they went out
> quickly from the tomb with fear and great joy and ran
> to bring His disciples word.
> – MATHEW 28:5–8

# His Name

Jesus!
Lord Jesus!
I love to say Your name!
Your ruddy complexion
Crimson through
Confirms my life
Captured
By You

Jesus!
Lord Jesus!
I love to say Your name
Like kids set free to skip and play
Beckoned, captured, called
Absolutely delightful!
My everything!
My all!

*The name of the LORD is a strong tower;*
*the righteous run to it and are safe.*
*– PROVERBS 18:10*

# ALL FOR HIM

Make my ears light with hearing
Your scent
Quickly discerned
My eyes ache…

The dew
Of the mountain
Filling the cup
…to see You

The impulse that nourishes every cell
The fiber that binds
The Word that sustains
The peace that endures
Yoked with You upon this mountain
I find my deepest rest

*Behold, the LORD's hand is not shortened, that it cannot save;*
*nor His ear heavy, that it cannot hear.*
*– ISAIAH 59:1*

# First Clue

You cannot know
What God is teaching you
Unless you know
What He has already taught you.

I am not really fond of mystery novels—at least I don't take time to read a lot of them. But I am compelled to uncover mystery: to use clues I have about God to find out more about God. I can't get enough.

It used to bother me to hear that in the parable of the talents and money, one servant gets a bunch, another a little. The one who uses or invests gets even more. The one who hides or hordes had it taken away! I felt sorry for the poor guy who ended up with nothing.

*"And he said to those who stood by, 'Take the mina from him, and give it to him who has ten minas. (But they said to him, 'Master, he has ten minas.')*
*– LUKE 19:24–25*

But maybe Jesus is talking about more than talent or money. Maybe He is also talking about a kernel of God revelation that He gives to each of us in order to find Him. Perhaps He is hinting, "I am here and I want to be found!" Finding Him leads to a greater understanding of Him, if we keep pursuing the clues laid out for us.

*For if you believed Moses, you would believe Me; for he wrote about Me. But if you do not believe his writings, how will you believe My words?"*
*– JOHN 5:46–47*

# GROW

I don't want
To live
A life
Unchallenged
And sit
Smugly
In old brine

*By which have been given to us exceedingly great and precious
promises, that through these you may be partakers of the divine
nature, having escaped the corruption that is in the world through
lust. But also, for this very reason, giving all diligence, add to
your faith virtue, to virtue knowledge, to knowledge self-control,
to self-control perseverance, to perseverance godliness, to god-
liness brotherly kindness, and to brotherly kindness love. For if
these things are yours and abound, you will be neither barren nor
unfruitful in the knowledge of our Lord Jesus Christ.*

– 2 PETER 1:4–8

# DEEP WITHIN

Is anything too small for You to notice? To nurture?
Does any detail escape Your invested view?
Can I hide from Your mercy and love?

Alleluia!
What a Savior, Whose redemption's reach
Extends to the conscience crippled by sin!
Restoring, sanctifying
Deep within
'Til all that's left of me is pure—
The very love of God endures.
Everywhere His eye can see Redemptive Blood!
I am set free!

*Therefore, He is also able to save to the uttermost those
who come to God through Him, since He always lives to
make intercession for them.*
*– HEBREWS 7:25*

*"Most assuredly, I say to you, he who hears My word and believes
in Him who sent Me has everlasting life, and shall not come into
judgment, but has passed from death into life."*
*– JOHN 5:24*

# A "LIKE YOU" LIFE

Father, take my mind, my heart, my all
Freely given, received, returned
Cast out "Look at me" thoughts and
Fill me with "Look at You" thoughts
And "Look at You" actions
Today
This minute
The remaining expanse
Of my life.

*Then Jesus answered and said to them,*
*"Most assuredly, I say to you, the Son can do nothing of Himself,*
*but what He sees the Father do; for whatever He does,*
*the Son also does in like manner."*
*– JOHN 5:19*

# Beside Within

There is nothing I desire
In heaven or on earth
Grateful to be near You
Celebrate Your worth
The counsel from Your mouth
As I spend time with You today
The Word of God my map and guide
Breathes life into this clay
You walk beside within me
I walk in faith abroad
Miraculous in every way
This covenant of God

*"This is the covenant that I will make with them after those days,*
*says the Lord: I will put My laws into their hearts, and in their*
*minds I will write them," then He adds, "Their sins and their*
*lawless deeds I will remember no more."*
*– Hebrews 10:16–17*

# GENTLED

*When they went, I heard the noise of their wings,*
*like the noise of many waters, like the voice of the Almighty,*
*a tumult like the noise of an army; and when they stood still,*
*they let down their wings.*
*– EZEKIEL 1:24*

Father, when You spoke to Ezekiel, You sounded so overwhelmingly mighty. He says, "As the noise of great waters, and the voice as the sound of a host." (Amplified Bible) The roaring of Your words could not be refused or denied, the vision so tremendous, even greater than any human imagination.

*"And remained astonished among them for seven days."*
*– EZEKIEL 3:15*

He must have been astonished, all right! What a vision!

When You come to me, Your voice is so subtle, the vision so hidden and shaded from view. There is more likelihood that I will miss it completely than know it with certainty. Often You approach me repeatedly before I even recognize that You are speaking to me. Why is that?

Help me not to be critical of Your way. It is best. But, let me not fail to recognize its importance. Let me glean all I can in finding Your reasons for communicating to me the way You do. Your subtlety can be distressing in that I desperately don't want to miss You. The world shouts to be heard. The clamoring patterns of my own thoughts have been long trained in a propensity toward selfish, worldly ways. I war against them to hear Your Holy Spirit's voice. Oh Lord! I don't want to miss You!

Your gentle way with me maintains my equilibrium better, doesn't it? You gently lead me. I depend on You not to lose me in the crowded space of my life. I'm listening for Your voice. I'm watching for Your presence. Your movement. Savior, like a shepherd, lead me!

*My sheep hear My voice,*
*and I know them, and they follow Me.*
*– JOHN 10:27*

*However, when He, the Spirit of truth, has come,*
*He will guide you into all truth; for He will not speak on*
*His own authority, but whatever He hears He will speak;*
*and He will tell you things to come.*
*– JOHN 16:13*

# CONVINCED

She is as a woman
Who stands at the door
Looking for her Beloved
Ready to open it
When He comes

She KNOWS
He's coming

*In My Father's house are many mansions; if it were not so,*
*I would have told you. I go to prepare a place for you. And if I go*
*and prepare a place for you, I will come again and receive you to*
*Myself; that where I am, there you may be also.*

*– JOHN 14:2–3*

# THE CROSS

I am captured today by a certain horror, a real horror, a "for sure" horror: the horror of the cross.

What price did Jesus pay for me? At what cost did He purchase my redemption? We have seen on TV some of the vilest of human hatred. We have read accounts of the atrocities of war too awful to grasp. We have seen Satan wage war against humanity through men in the most despicable and heinously murderous ways. He is destroyer of all that is good. Yet for all that we could possibly read or experience, Jesus suffered more. His dear body was so shattered that it was unrecognizable.

It was because of sin, my sin, that He endured that. Indeed, it was Jesus, the Lamb prepared for slaughter from the beginning of time, the perfect, loving Darling of the Father, reserved for such a thing. Crucifixion for my redemption. The depth of His voluntary sacrifice so I could be free is beyond, way beyond, what can be accurately depicted.

Even more than can be physically, mentally, or emotionally imagined was the depth of His agony. You, Father, turned away from Him. Jesus was abandoned by His friends, but oh! Depth of anguish! He was abandoned by You! My heart reels and pitches with quaking at the thought of Him being separated from You! You were His connection as He walked this sinful earth. You were His vision, His comfort, and His friend. He did only what He saw You do.

Heaven's most cherished One looked to You for all things. And when He had gathered all the sin, every disease and sickness and the poverty of the world on His once beautiful, now shredded body, He must have looked to You for approval. He must have hungered for Your voice of benediction on what He had done. But instead He saw You had looked away and forsaken Him. Oh! Oh! Oh! my heart!

*Just as many were astonished at you,*
*So His visage was marred more than any man,*
*And His form more than the sons of men.*
*– ISAIAH 52:14*

Father, in Your Mercy You held back the scene of this horror engulfing Jesus by causing darkness to obscure our vision. Evil covered the land and there was laughter at the gates of hell. But oh, what a morning that followed, when the grave could not hold Him! The covenant was fulfilled, the letter of the law sealed. The perfect life lived and sacrificed to free me! The perfect life! Lived, sacrificed, raised from the dead, and gloriously approved and revealed by You.

*Now when the sixth hour had come, there was darkness over*
*the whole land until the ninth hour. And at the ninth hour*
*Jesus cried out with a loud voice, saying, "Eloi, Eloi, lama*
*sabachthani?" which is translated, "My God, My God,*
*why have you forsaken me?"*
*– MARK 15:33–34*

*But he said to them, "Do not be alarmed. You seek Jesus of*
*Nazareth, who was crucified. He is risen! He is not here.*
*See the place where they laid Him."*
*– MARK 16:6*

# LITTLE CROSS

What cross is this
Little cross
Puny cross
And what this table
Of sacrifice
On which I am to lie

Why the squeal
Of complaint
Oh my soul

In the shadow
Of His
Cross
I carry no weight
His yoke is easy
His burden is light

*Come to me, all you who labor and are heavy laden, and I will
give you rest. Take my yoke upon you, and learn of me, for I am
gentle and lowly in heart, and you will find rest for your souls. For
my yoke is easy and my burden is light.*
*– MATTHEW 11:28–30*

# WHAT JOY

*Looking unto Jesus, the author and finisher of our faith, who for*
*the joy that was set before Him endured the cross, despising the*
*shame, and has sat down at the right hand of the throne of God.*
*– HEBREWS 12:2*

Oh, the height and depth and length and width of the love of God for His creation! Plumbing the depths and searching the extent of that love will ever be my delight. My heart trips over itself in gratitude, joy, and love for Him. Seeking to delight my Father's heart is my daily sonorous occupation, the Holy Spirit providing rhythm and harmony to the melody God has put in me.

Ocean resounding
Mountains ringing
Canyons echoing
Thunderstorms singing
The earth a wave
Offering
First fruits of a mighty throng
Pulsating, growing
Bursting in new
Ancient song

Nature compelling
Children forth telling
Songs loud and clear
Ancient and near

God's mighty calling'
Past slumber awakening
A mighty victorious
Army all glorious

Christ rises to reign
Giving gifts unto men
Cast doubt far away
Stand strong in the fray
Use freely the sword
Your weapon of war
Let fear and sin tremble
God's army stands firm
The joy set before them
The strength that endures

Satan confused
Why all the dancing?
My roaring and threatening
Stomping and prancing
See me
Look at me
Waving and yelling
Look at ME
See ME

But no one would

Our vision held captive
By one risen King
Ruler all glorious
THAT'S why we sing!

# SPARROWS

The sparrows on my dad's farm were quite a nuisance in the barn. They flew around the low ceiling, building nests in the rafters and making a mess in general, multiplying in numbers 'til there were just too many.

We children would take the BB gun after chores in the evening, grab a flashlight and hunt, shoot, and deliver dead sparrows for a penny a piece to Dad and then throw them to the cats. We thought nothing of the sparrows, only of the growing cache of pennies.

One of the basic problems regarding our relationship with our heavenly Father is we limit Him in our thoughts to being kind of like us. Who of us takes personal concern for each of the hairs on our own head? Okay. Maybe for our own hair, but for the hair of others? It is unlikely we would caringly and tenderly count them!

The Father has! Each and every hair on my head is numbered by Him. Accurately! Each sparrow that has ever fallen He knows. Each wild flower—most of which human eye will never even see—He has clothed with care and pleasure.

Oh, we do Him a disservice by receiving only a little of His love for us when He has such tremendous love to give! We don't really believe that He can or that He wants to passionately love us.

None of us deserve it. That much we can recognize and He already and certainly knows. But it is who He is. There is no edge to the measure of His love for us.

HE IS LOVE.

Unfortunately, we restrict the flow of His love with our own narrow belief and understanding of His character. We may have, in faith, received salvation. We may have accepted His help in getting us out of some besetting sin. But what about the blistering headache that keeps coming back?

Or the empty checkbook? The anger or impatience that erupts? My life couldn't be something He wants to help me with because He is too busy keeping me saved, right? Salvation is my portion and that's about it. I'd better be satisfied with salvation and a trip to heaven when I die. After all, that's big! He must have blown His whole wad in that truly huge gift.

NOT!

Jesus did a real number to sin on the cross. He licked it once and for all. He paid the whole price for us. Now we have redemption and though we remain in a struggle, our home in heaven has been secured. But...

Jesus wasn't the Father's wad! The cross certainly was necessary for salvation. But it was not the end or the limit of His love for us. The action of the love of the Father was clear long before the cross and continues long after. The flow from His heart never quits.

Jesus came and showed us the Father's love in the obedient life and death He lived. In Him there is a perfect *Yes* to our every need.

*Are not two sparrows sold for a copper coin? And not one of them falls to the ground apart from your Father's will. But the very hairs on your head are numbered. Do not fear therefore; you are of more value than many sparrows.*

– Matthew 10:29–31

*For all the promises of God in Him are Yes, and in Him Amen, to the glory of God through us.*

– 2 Corinthians 1:20

# FULLNESS

Oh boy, do we need miraculous salvation! We cannot have life unless we believe Jesus' substitutionary death brings it to us. Do we need the same miraculous healing? Oh, we can get by without that. We'll just hobble around wincing from pain, choosing to put on a smile and face the music of a crippled future. Many say that kind of healing is not for today.

Do we think that God does not want us well? Deep down inside us, God birthed a *knowing* that He wants us whole and well in our bodies. Why else would we spend our hard-earned money on endless remedies? Why struggle against God if He does not want us well? We know there is more to the salvation message than spiritual redemption. We see a covenant completed by God in Jesus:

> *Therefore, if anyone is in Christ, he is a new creation;*
> *old things have passed away; behold, all things have become new.*
> *– II Corinthians 5:17*

Man cannot imagine what God has in store for those who love Him. What part of the price for our complete redemption did Jesus *not* pay for? What part did He withhold that we should not have the good things that God promised in the old covenant? And now an even better covenant!

> *For if by the one man's offense death reigned through the one,*
> *much more those who receive abundance of grace and of the gift of*
> *righteousness will reign in life through the One, Jesus Christ.*
> *– Romans 5:17*

One man—Jesus—brought life that all might live. Do we receive His free gift? Not only part, but the whole? Has Satan hoodwinked us into believing that he still has the right to lock us up, that he still has parts of us he can mess with?

Not so, according to Jesus. He took the key to prison away from Satan at the cross. Satan no longer has the right to lock us up in poverty or constrict us with lack. He has no authority to bind us in illness. NO. The key has been taken back by Jesus. He has authority over us. He dwells in us. We belong to Him.

Father, you alone can know how much I struggle to maintain faith in your full and complete redemptive covenant. Your death, Lord Jesus, certainly paid the price in full for my healing, spirit, soul, and body. I have had a taste of the kingdom of God and know that it is good and is what I want. Here. Now.

You have a perspective that I can only glimpse. Although I want to walk in the fullness of Your kingdom, I am very limited in what I think that means. My body hurts and I want the healing I know You accomplished for me on the cross. You want my complete holiness. I so often want what pleases *me* most.

In You, Jesus, I have a sure and living hope. All the promises in You are yes and amen. I claim them now in joyful expectant hope, through struggle, pain, and difficulties. I know You are true. Your mercies are new every morning. Great, so great, is Your faithfulness.

# STIR IT UP

God isn't wearied by His interest
In every hair on my head
Or accurate account of every living bird.

He is always giving all
He says what He means
He means what He says.

Listen to God's heart
Though many are ignorant
the kindness of God is unrelenting.

God's great love extends to all
Stir up the gift of love within You.
Find it.
Nurture it.
Think it.
Express it.
Grab it.
Enjoy it.
Feed it.
Release it.
Flow with it.
Be anointed with it.
Dance
With grit
Lord, let me know and express Your heart.

*But be doers of the word, and not hearers only,*
*deceiving yourselves.*
*– JAMES 1:22*

# Upright and Firm

Those who love Me shall stand
Upright
Firm
Those who seek Me will find Me
Early
Those who know Me shall do
Exploits

Because the Father rules His kingdom judging right from wrong in truth and love, with mercy, peace, and joy, so should we. He has turned the care of His kingdom over to us. We reign with Him.

Put on your fine garments
Your King draws nigh
At the very door
We stand
God arrives
His enemies are scattered

*Those who do wickedly against the covenant he shall corrupt with flattery; but the people who know their God shall be strong, and carry out great exploits.*
*– DANIEL 11:32*

# CHOSEN

Birthright sold
Despised
Rejected

Second born
Blessed
Promised heaven

God
Of second chances
In mercy moves

Prodigal returns
Reborn
Forgiven

Family regained
Not one or two
Three

God within
Whole for eternity

*Therefore consider the goodness and severity of God: on those
who fell, severity; but toward you, goodness, if you continue
in his goodness. Otherwise you also will be cut off. And they also,
if they do not continue in unbelief, will be grafted in,
for God is able to graft them in again.*
*– ROMANS 11:22–23*

# Birthright Sold

*But Jacob said, "Sell me your birthright as of this day." And Esau*
*said, "Look, I am about to die; so what is this birthright to me?"*
*Then Jacob said, "Swear to me as of this day." So he swore to him,*
*and sold his birthright to Jacob. And Jacob gave Esau bread and*
*stew of lentils; then he ate and drank, arose, and went his way.*
*Thus Esau despised his birthright.*
*– Genesis 25:31–34*

A birthright is a very valuable thing. To turn over the blessings of the first-born is to despise the best gifts. *(But earnestly desire the best gifts. – 1 Corinthians 12:31)*

This best gift has been taken from Israel. The Jews despised Jesus, their birthright, and as a consequence the blessing was turned over from them to the Church.

We should earnestly desire and seek the advantage that has, for a time, come to us. If we seek, we shall surely find.

Jealousy shall spring up from a nation robbed of their rightful blessing; godly jealousy for what is rightfully theirs, diligent searching and struggle against sin, anguish of heart, tears flowing like a river over the lost Lamb of Israel. The firstborn shall yet seek God and return to receive their full blessing.

*"And I will pour on the house of David and on the inhabitants*
*of Jerusalem the Spirit of grace and supplication; then they will*
*look on Me whom they pierced. Yes, they will mourn for Him*

*as one mourns for his only son, and grieve for Him as one*
*grieves for a firstborn."*
– ZECHARIAH 12:10

Weep my beloved
Weep
For you shall yet reap a harvest
Of blessing

*"In that day a fountain shall be opened for the house of David and*
*for the inhabitants of Jerusalem, for sin and for uncleanness.*
– ZECHARIAH 13:1

# GRAFTED

Read Romans Chapters 9, 10, and 11.

This scripture speaks clearly to the time of the Gentiles, grafted into the living vine while for a time the Israelites are cut off. Jesus, Jewish himself, born to save His people, was rejected and crucified. The Jews said no to God's plan of redemption, having long before selected their own way over His.

But as Jesus' example of the Prodigal Son, the Father is ever extending mercy with a watchful eye to His son's return. In the meantime, the blessing of the Gentiles flow in part to stir up jealousy.

> *But I say, did Israel not know? First Moses says: "I will provoke*
> *you to jealousy by those who are not a nation, I will move*
> *you to anger by a foolish nation.*
> *– ROMANS 10:19*

> *I say then, have they stumbled that they should fall?*
> *Certainly not! But through their fall, to provoke them*
> *to jealousy, salvation has come to the Gentiles.*
> *– ROMANS 10:11*

"Jealous" is a way God describes Himself.

> *For you shall worship no other god, for the LORD,*
> *whose name is Jealous, is a jealous God,*
> *– EXODUS 34:14*

God wants a people who will depend on Him and no other; who will worship Him and no other; who will serve Him and no other; who will love and adore Him and no other. A people who will value a relationship with Him above all else. His acts of love long to land on a people who look to Him and lean on Him. He is jealous of where our devotion is. He wants it to be on Him. He is worthy. None other is. He wants the best for us. None other does.

God will not fail to stay true to His Name and character. He is jealous for His chosen and will not change.

*For the gifts and the calling of God are irrevocable.*
– ROMANS 11:29

# New Year's Solutions

This year, instead of making yet another set of New Year's resolutions, I felt compelled to write a different kind of list. It is entitled, "What I need God to do for me that I have tried to do, over and over in the past, and am unable to accomplish." Most of the items on the list are of little importance and would be overlooked as insignificant to the world (though I don't know a single woman who doesn't want to get rid of cellulite). But for me, turning some simple though undoable things over to the Lord has given me immense freedom and rest. Peace comes every time I remember they are no longer my concern but are on God's to-do list. My job is to keep my nose out of His business.

*Come to Me, all you who labor and are heavy laden, and I will*
*give you rest. Take My yoke upon you and learn from Me,*
*for I am gentle and lowly in heart, and you will find rest for*
*your souls. For My yoke is easy and My burden is light.*
*– Matthew 11:28–30*

# MODERATION

I am discovering incredible enjoyment in my life of God-sanctioned and God-empowered moderation. Absolutely no glory in the flesh in this. Oh no, I would rather God had said, "No more sweets!" and "No more beer or wine!" and "No more TV!" and even "No more naps!" But alleluia! He said all things are redeemed unto Him and by Him and given to us for our great enjoyment, entertainment, and pleasure. He so delights to give us every good thing!

My great revelation came like flipping on a switch. When He has told me to fast, His strength to do it was always at the ready. Suddenly, I realized that when He tells me "all things in moderation to enjoy!" His power to curb my addictive personality and liberate my guilt-bound conscience is also available. Duh!?

Thank You, Lord! My prideful flesh can rear its head in strict discipline of do's don'ts, but not in the liberty of Your moderating power!

*Now the Spirit expressly says that in latter times some will depart from the faith, giving heed to deceiving spirits and doctrines of demons...*

*– 1 TIMOTHY 4:1*

*Forbidding to marry, and commanding to abstain from foods which God created to be received with thanksgiving by those who believe and know the truth. For every creature of God is good, and nothing is to be refused if it is received with thanksgiving; for it is sanctified by the word of God and prayer.*

*– 1 TIMOTHY 4:3–5*

# LOCKED OUT

For the second time in recent days, I found myself locked out. The first time I left the car running and went to brush snow off of it and found the doors all locked up! But it was just parked outside the garage, and in the house I found the second set of keys and was able to open the car door. Very thankful! This morning I went out to the garage freezer to get something to thaw for supper and the house door was locked. Fortunately, the front door was unlocked and I got back in the house.

So, Lord, I am thankful for a way to get back inside, but I also want to hear Your comments. This having happened twice You have my attention.

When the heavens seem to be brass and the way thoroughly blocked, does it mean that I do not see? Have I eyes of brass or ears of wood that I cannot see or hear?

"I made wood. I made brass! The trees bow in My presence and brass melts. I put ears on the waves of the seas and they listen to me. Though the heavens be unsearchable and the way closed and hard, know that I am as near as your breath. One way may be blocked; another will surely open. I, the Lord, will perform it."

Thank You, Father, for Your way is my only way. Though one door may be closed and anther open, Your Word remains a lamp to my feet and a light to my path. Help me to hear You in every situation. You unlock the solution to my every need. I love You.

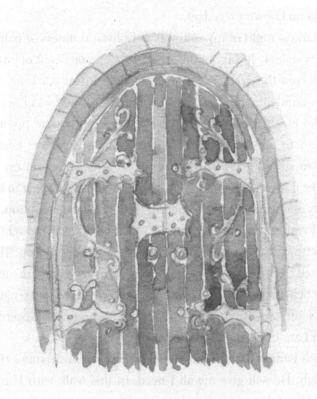

*Your word is a lamp to my feet*
*And a light to my path.*
– PSALM 119:105

# Darkest Night

Sometimes the way God tests our faith is to bring us to a place where there is no known precedent.

The darkest night of my soul was not physical illness or pain. It was not poverty or lack. It was not the loneliness of being bereft of loved ones. It was not even the deep chasm of depression. It was when my Self as a precious, confident, and dependable source of council was knocked out from under me. Self proved so wrong that credibility went up in flames, never again to appear trustworthy. My countenance was beaten as I walked through my days with the weight of this corpse on my back. It seemed like it took a long time for the wind of the Holy Spirit to blow the ashes away and for the Word of God to wash me in regeneration.

Now I realize that nothing short of death could have brought me life. I no longer have Self to fall back on, much less to depend on. The ashes are scattered over the kingdom and I pray my martyrdom, my life freely given, my Self burnt for the love of my Lord, will serve to strengthen the brethren. I am left with no source other than Jesus and His Spirit within me ... and I am in need of no other.

Though I am only beginning to hear Him and understand His ways, it is enough. He will give me all I need. In this walk with Him comes liberty and confidence.

He is SURE. He is TRUTH. He is ABLE. I am crucified with Christ, therefore I no longer live but Jesus Christ now lives in me! Alleluia! Glory!

*I have been crucified with Christ; it is no longer I who live, but
Christ lives in me; and the life which I now live in the flesh
I live by faith in the Son of God,
who loved me and gave Himself for me.*

– GALATIANS 2:20

# HE WOULD HAVE

He would have.
He really would have.
Oh, yes. His love is that unfathomable.

He would have suffered the cross, as many times as there are stars in the heavens, to win me to Himself and the Father. He would have done whatever the Father required to redeem me, to redeem each of us.

But the Father said once was enough. He sent His Son to do the complete job. Jesus held nothing back in His sacrifice for us. He did all that was required for my soul that one time on the cross. The law was fulfilled in Him. Fully filled. Every 't' crossed, every 'i' dotted. The perfect Lamb of God sent to take away the entire sin of the world.

The Father sent from heaven
The perfect Grip
His pierced hand
Encircled the neck
Of the evil one
Held him to the
Ground
And stood upon him
With hammered feet
To crush
To strike the blow
His heel came down
The battle won

Vile to the grave went down
Borne upon a cross of scorn
Victory won!
My soul reborn!

*So when Jesus had received the sour wine, He said, "It is finished!"*
*And bowing His head, He gave up His spirit.*
*– JOHN 19:30*

# A LOVE SO GRAND

A love as big as God's love goes way beyond and before redemption. He did not only see our souls set free, though that was part of His joy. He also saw Satan defeated and all his children destroyed. He loved us so much, so freely and so vehemently that no evil formed against us can prosper. Every vile, contemptible, trouble-brewing spirit captured and brought to the grave, and Scripture even indicates that the grave is too good for them. Though the kings of the earth sleep in the graves of their glory, Satan will be spewed out of his and dragged to the very stones of the pit. He is so roundly defeated in Jesus that he and all his followers will never even be named! See Isaiah 14.

*All the kings of the nations,*
*All of them, sleep in glory,*
*Everyone in his own house;*
*But you are cast out of your grave*
*Like an abominable branch,*
*Like the garment of those who are slain,*
*Thrust through with a sword,*
*Who go down to the stones of the pit,*
*Like a corpse trodden underfoot.*
*You will not be joined with them in burial,*
*Because you have destroyed your land*
*And slain your people.*
*The brood of evildoers shall never be named.*
*– ISAIAH 14:18–20*

God hates the enemy of His people. He protects and provides victory for us in Jesus. A love so grand that we are given authority to speak to every mountain that hinders us and every evil that confronts us. We can rightfully call them bought down and powerless.

*"No weapon formed against you shall prosper,*
*And every tongue which rises against you in judgment*
*You shall condemn.*
*This is the heritage of the servants of the LORD,*
*And their righteousness is from Me," says the LORD.*

– ISAIAH 54:17

His is a love so grand that He gives the Holy Spirit to each of us and brings the truth of God's Word to our hearts. He empowers us for the present battle against our foe. He instructs and prepares us for what lies ahead. He takes us to Himself and, as a father, loves us.

Be hungry. Be teachable. Be children of God, eager to hear His voice and follow His leading. His love is heard in His Word, breathed so full of truth and love for us. It is capable of washing us, nourishing us, guiding us and living in us. God's Word imparts life.

We begin to understand Him and oh! He wants us to get to know Him! There is no limit to what He wants to impart to us!

His love is so grand
Like a big brass band
On every corner
And more
More
More

# UPTURNED POTS

Read II Kings 2:1–7.

I think of that woman Elisha ministered to. How many upturned pots can I present to the Lord that He might fill? How needy am I? Very! How hungry? Starved! He will only stop pouring when I run out of capacity.

> Will I dare to believe it?
> Do I dare say yes?
> To believe and receive
> That my joy
> Might be full?
> So generous!
> So sure!
> So unrestricted!
> Such a longing
> To give His best!

I want the container of my capacity to be leaking all over the place. I want the oil of His Spirit to be a life source to all He brings my way.

The fact that He wants to share His glory with and through us doesn't surprise me. He isn't like us! He has no limit. That He shares His glory with us only magnifies Him in my eyes.

Alleluia! What a wonder! What a joy!

*"I do not pray for these alone, but also for those who will believe*
*in Me through their word; that they all may be one, as You,*
*Father, are in Me, and I in You; that they also may be one in Us,*
*that the world may believe that You sent Me. And the glory which*

*You gave Me I have given them, that they may be one just as We are one." I in them, and You in Me; that they may be made perfect in one, and that the world may know that You have sent Me, and have loved them as You have loved Me.*

– JOHN 17:20–23

# BATTLE RAGES

There are several areas in which Satan battles for our lives and our spirits. The spirit is the first that needs to be won. Unless we are born again, we cannot go on even recognizing the others.

*Jesus answered and said to him, "Most assuredly, I say to you,*
*unless one is born again, he cannot see the kingdom of God."*
*– JOHN 3:3*

Satan's primary purpose has and always will be to drag God's created children into eternal death with him. He would conquer there first. He knows the truth of God's gift of life to us better than we do. He knows that once that sin nature is put to the cross of Jesus, the other areas of battle fall like dominoes out of his court. He has lost, totally.

That does not mean, however, that he loses the war for our spirits with grace or dignity, accepting, defeat. Oh, no! He kicks and squeals like a pig going to slaughter. True to his vicious nature, he strikes like a viper to poison us if he can. And often he does.

Our minds become the next battleground of choice. Much has been written on the battle for the believers' mind. Ephesians tells of our armor and weapons quite clearly. None needs to stand naked in the battlefield.

*Therefore take up the whole armor of God, that you may be able*
*to withstand in the evil day, and having done all, to stand.*
*– EPHESIANS 6:13*

The Holy Spirit joins us in a most powerful way to equip us for victory. That does not easily accomplish it, however. There is a battle raging, but the renewed mind is the victorious mind. The Word planted in the soil of the mind, watered, cultivated, and fertilized frequently is the mind that produces a harvest of life. We cannot take our responsibility in this lightly. It is up to us to receive and nurture the Word delivered. When the Spirit recreates our dead spirits with His life, we become perceptive to the Word of Life. When we hear it, when we see it, if we read it, it penetrates like it couldn't before. The Spirit urges us to receive it and tend it.

At first it may be, and should be, a brand-new joy! So alive in the promises of God! Such Truth to set us free! Such wisdom! A rich banquet to which He invites us to be renewed to a whole new way of thinking! The Holy Spirit brings just the right Word of nourishment to fill us and yet causes us to hunger for more. It is this "hungering for more," this Godly jealousy for belonging to the One True God, that longs to be recognized and nurtured. It should unsettle us enough to seek God.

What do we do with the Manna He delivers? Do we treat it as refuse? Do we tuck it away for later use, only to be distracted and forget about it? (Wouldn't that please Satan!?) Or do we receive it, chew on it, digest all we can from it until the next course is served up?

Does it make us satisfied and content? Or do we relish it, stirring up hunger for more? If we don't, we do not trust or know the greatness of God and the banquet He invites us to. Oh, there is so much more!

Renewing our minds brings with it the opportunity for physical renewal as well.

> *But those who wait on the LORD*
> *Shall renew their strength;*
> *They shall mount up with wings like eagles,*
> *They shall run and not be weary,*
> *They shall walk and not faint.*
> *– ISAIAH 40:31*

We have untapped potential here for indescribable wellness, but Satan, as a roaring lion, will try to prevent the rest that God has promised us. He would prefer that we remain ignorant of Jesus' accomplishment for our healing. But if he can't keep the true Word from us, he will make it look false! Ugh! We are so crippled by walking by sight and what we feel that we fail to receive the solid sure promises of God.

The battle rages. It truly does. Our flesh walks this sinful earth, and we have been taught that complete healing and wholeness can be obtained only beyond the grave. Scripture certainly reveals completeness in His presence in heaven, but the last enemy to be defeated will be/is death.

> *He will swallow up death forever,*
> *And the Lord GOD will wipe away tears from all faces;*
> *The rebuke of His people*
> *He will take away from all the earth;*
> *For the LORD has spoken.*
> *– ISAIAH 25:8*

> *For He must reign till He has put all enemies under His feet. The*
> *last enemy that will be destroyed is death.*
> *– 1 CORINTHIANS 15:25–26*

That seems to mean there is an awful lot of life to live before death transports us. And the scripture indicates some may not die before the Lord's return.

> *Then we who are alive and remain shall be caught up together*
> *with them in the clouds to meet the Lord in the air. And thus we*
> *shall always be with the Lord.*
> *-1 THESSALONIANS 4:17*

Eternal Life begins for us when we are born again by the Spirit of God. As we walk toward God in that benevolent path He has laid out for us, we have every right as His children to claim the Kingdom now. His reward is with Him. There is no part of this reward that cannot bless us now. God bears the physical answer as He does the spiritual and mental.

> *There remains therefore a rest for the people of God. For he who*
> *has entered His rest has himself also ceased from his works as God*
> *did from His. Let us therefore be diligent to enter that rest, lest*
> *anyone fall according to the same example of disobedience.*
> – HEBREWS 4:9–11

The world has ways it convinces us to gain physical strength, health, and beauty. We are fools to believe it. The ways of the world are so far from the ways of God they are ridiculous. God says,

> *"For My thoughts are not your thoughts,*
> *Nor are your ways My ways," says the LORD.*
> *"For as the heavens are higher than the earth,*
> *So are My ways higher than your ways,*
> *And My thoughts than your thoughts."*
> – ISAIAH 55:8

He seems to indicate that waiting and rest are His solutions for strength and beauty. With quietness and confidence comes your radiant beauty. Why do we labor for that which we cannot possibly obtain through our own effort? Because Satan is successfully fooling us! The more effort we put into the saving of our bodies, the less we have the time and energy to wait and rest in the Lord! He will renew our strength. Our effort will not. It will only make us weary and discouraged as we come to its dead end, a dismal future for the flesh to be sure.

Let us not limit God in this body of flesh He has prepared for us. As we hear the truth, let us grab hold of the labor that brings us rest. We need to be obedient to Him and Him alone. We need to make the choice "All for God."

The Word of God is clearly calling us to live His way. The world tickles us with flesh-gratifying ways. There is much poisonous pride in all of it. Struggle out of the sequined pretense of its robe and snuggle into the garment of humility. God's Word is true. There is a deep rest for the people of God! Let us choose His way.

As we follow in the footsteps of our risen Lord, let us look for help in all of these areas, to the Scriptures, the Body of Christ, and the help of the Holy Spirit.

> *Therefore, since a promise remains of entering His rest,*
> *let us fear lest any of you seem to have come short of it.*
> – HEBREWS 4:1

# POINTING TO JESUS

*Let God be true and every man a liar.*
*– ROMANS 3:4.*

The blessings of God for His people, though completed in Jesus, are not fully apparent. Just because we don't see those blessings in the flesh doesn't mean they have not been accomplished.

*For now we see in a mirror, dimly, but then face to face. Now I*
*know in part, but then I shall know just as I also am known.*
*– 1 CORINTHIANS 13:12*

Our view into the spirit world is a peek at best. The arrow of focus from our gracious God points, always points, to Jesus. He was and ever is established as the manifest presence of God. In Him dwells the fullness of God.

For this reason, we can be confident we will never completely tap the depths of these blessings. We do not yet see all of them prepared for us, as is evident by our own need. But we can with assurance petition the Father for them. He invites us to ask boldly. Ask for what? All that He has to offer!

*Every good gift and every perfect gift is from above, and comes*
*down from the Father of lights, with whom there is no variation*
*or shadow of turning.*
*– JAMES 1:17*

*For the LORD God is a sun and shield;*
*The LORD will give grace and glory;*
*No good thing will He withhold from*
*those who walk uprightly.*
– PSALM 84:11

# STILL SCUFFED

*"I am the true vine, and My Father is the vinedresser.*
*Every branch in Me that does not bear fruit He takes away;*
*and every branch that bears fruit He prunes,*
*that it may bear more fruit."*
– JOHN 15:1–2

Now THAT opens up a pack of blessings!

During this time of courtship, before Jesus comes to receive His pure, spotless Bride, we are being washed and pressed. The scripture clearly indicates that He uses testing and trial to grow us in godly character and holiness. Victory should be manifested in our lives with increasing clarity. If there is some affliction in our lives, we should be submitting to Him for pruning. Misfortune will be used by God for our benefit…

*And we know that all things work together for good to them that*
*love God, to them who are the called according to his purpose.*
– ROMANS 8:28

He will not withhold His blessing even within that difficulty, in the very blackest part. His love constrains Him to deliver that which we have need of.

Right now, in this page of history, we need a bit of "polish" to prepare for Jesus' coming.

# THE PRUNING SHED

There is a place of sacrifice the Lord has taken me to time and time again. In my mind's eye, there is a door I might go through ... or run from.

The first time I ventured through that door there appeared a small simple, intimate room; in the middle of it, a table of sorts. I knew it was important for me to lie upon this table and submit to God. "You are the vine. I am the husbandman" clearly sprang up in my heart, from John 15:1–2. I knew I could trust this dear Gardener, and I became certain that it was in my best interest that I submit to His pruning knife. Entering that room the first few times was so hard. I dreaded the knife. But always the Father made such clean cuts; though each was painful, His hand also delivered healing. It was a good thing to be still in His sculpting hands.

Over the years, we have met often in that room of sacrifice. It has become a place I treasure and am eager to return to. Though it is a place where the blood freely flows, I would rather die than miss the full flow of His life in me.

The Father has the whole picture. He knows where to start, where to stop, where to increase, and where to decrease. He is preparing a "body" for His dear Son that is befitting a King. What part of beauty should we not claim? What part of sin should He not require us to let go? What part of sinful nature not expunged?

We have promises from a God who is love. He is ready to work in us and eager to work through us every good thing. We belong to a God who is personal. He meets us on a first-name basis. He simply cannot stop caring. What a treasure we bear in these earthen vessels!

We are embraced from the inside by a God who would never violate us. He merely wants our love. Those who obey His commands are those who love Him.

With what part of "Love the Lord your God with all your heart, mind, soul, and strength" and "Love your neighbor as yourself" are we needing help? God knows best what we require to unfold the best in us. We are told in Scripture to come boldly and ask. But sometimes we just don't know what's best for us. The Holy Spirit does. It is perfectly clear to Him what we need and what the Father's desired outcome is for us.

The fruits of the Spirit as we abide in the vine should be prolific in our lives. Evident. That means the neighbors should be able to see them. If any of those fruits are not blossoming and bearing, we need pruning! Ask for help. He is calling you to the pruning shed to treat you to a time of intimacy and tenderness. He yearns for this time with you and knows your deepest needs. The climate is right for God to accelerate His work in us. Don't waste the time resisting His promptings. Don't delay. Now is the time. Now is the hour. Hold nothing back in your climb upon that altar of sacrifice and He will hold nothing back from you.

*Therefore, as the Holy Spirit says: "Today, if you will hear*
*His voice, do not harden your hearts as in the rebellion,*
*in the day of trial in the wilderness.*
*– HEBREWS 3:7–8*

*But God has revealed them to us through His Spirit.*
*For the Spirit searches all things, yes, the deep things of God.*
*– 1 CORINTHIANS 2:10*

*Looking unto Jesus, the author and finisher of our faith, who for*
*the joy that was set before Him endured the cross, despising the*
*shame, and has sat down at the right hand of the throne of God.*
*– HEBREWS 12:2*

*But may the God of all grace, who called us to His eternal glory*
*by Christ Jesus, after you have suffered a while, perfect,*
*establish, strengthen, and settle you.*
— 1 PETER 5:10

# WEARY BONES

Father, "make these broken weary bones rise to dance again." Words from the song *Garment of Praise* by Jaime Harvill have become a prayer for Your church.

We are weary in our sin, plodding along in the uncomfortable effort to walk in the world whose ways are so treacherous and different from Christian life. We stray as hungry sheep looking for nourishment that will revive us. We need to return to the joy of our salvation, but we get stuck in the mire of wrong pastures. We call, pathetic, as we walk wearily along, stuck in the paths of our own making, our poor choices. Forgive us, Lord. We fix our eyes on You. Your way, Lord, is the right way. Help us. Take us by the bones and shake us free.

We want to be angry
We want to be unkind
Our tongues loosed in gossip
Backbiting

We want to do it our way
To please ourselves
We run from You
Resist You
Dig our feet in the mud
Hoping to find relief
From the wounds
Of walking the barbed paths
Of the world

Turn our heads
Fix our eyes on You
We are waiting
Drowning
Exhausted with self-effort
Getting nowhere
But more weary


Take us by our weary bones
Shake the oily mire of sin
That clings
We want to be back in Your arms
Wash us in Your mercy
Turn our heads
We are waiting
Pause ... sigh ... Selah


Stir the great compassion of Your heart
Til its flame roars with heat
To burn my sin
I hate it
Pause ... sigh ... Selah


Together with You
I will be thrown
Into the flaming inferno
Of your love
There
Plunged in the ocean of
Your glory
I will rise again
Pause ... sigh ... Selah

Bathed in Your glory
Covered in Your love
Ashes of wickedness
Blown away from above

Pause … sigh … Selah

*Then Jesus said to His disciples, "If anyone desires to come after Me, let him deny himself, and take up his cross, and follow Me.* [25] *For whoever desires to save his life will lose it, but whoever loses his life for My sake will find it.*

— MATTHEW 16:24–25

# DEEP CALLS TO DEEP

My eyes are fixed on You
The oil of gladness
Flows down
Like a river
Laughter like
Cherry blossoms
In spring

Thy billows have gone over me
My life is made new
Dearest High God
Keeper of Promises
My eyes are fixed on You

*Deep calls unto deep at the noise of Your waterfalls;*
*All Your waves and billows have gone over me.*
*– PSALM 42:7*

# DOWNSPOUTS

I remember standing beneath the drainpipe at home, rinsing my hair with the rainwater that gathered on the roof and collected to pour into and down the spout by the kitchen window. From it I received a soft clean refreshing in the rain.

There is still a blessing in it as I picture the water of God's Word gather on the curtains of my mind to collect and rinse away the old; softening, cleansing, comforting, and refreshing. All life formed in me by God in the past remains firm and nourished, while the old ways and things become a distant memory, washed away in a River of Life.

*And no one puts new wine into old wineskins; or else the new*
*wine bursts the wineskins, the wine is spilled, and the wineskins*
*are ruined. But new wine must be put into new wineskins.*
*– MARK 2:22*

# 'Rose from Bier

Again this day I take my cross
On which my soul does hang
So tough to keep that one upon
A bier so divine

For only death can keep me free
To live the Spirit's call
The cross becomes a sacred tool
To yield to Him my all

He raises me in righteousness
I stand before my Lord
He fills me with His strength and life
The Spirit's Word my sword

Prepared to move beyond the grave
Death is forever won
In life with joy I give my all
To Father
Spirit
Son

*Then He came and touched the bier, and those who carried him*
*stood still. And He said, "Young man, I say to you, arise."*
*– Luke 7:14*

# BUILT UPON THE ROCK

*Unless the LORD builds the house,*
*They labor in vain who build it;*
*Unless the LORD guards the city,*
*The watchman stays awake in vain.*

*– PSALM 127:1*

What kind of building material are we using for our own lives? There is no better material than the Word of God. There is nothing more accurate than that blueprint of instruction He has laid out for us in the Word. The revelation knowledge He brings, mingled with our faith in the Builder, makes structure out of it. All we have to do is hold on for the ride.

Refer to the blueprint often for insight and instruction and the house will stand. He is full of adventure and surprise in the quirkiness of His ways. He does not do what we would do or even what we think He would do.

So leave your nearsighted expectations and come anticipating a major blessing. Hold on. You will not be disappointed!

# Trust Him

God is all about giving us the desires of our hearts. He birthed many wonderful longings in our hearts so He could show Himself faithful, loving, and true.

How can we know if our desires fit His? We can't know what God is saying to us unless we know what He has already said. His Word discerns the thoughts and intents of our hearts. By it we know if we are responding to His desires in us, to some other passion ignited by ourselves and self-promoting motives, or to the evil one. If we are confirmed in the Word, we can have boldness to go to our prayer closets and demand the release of blessing and provision. God does not withhold good things from those who love Him.

If God who is faithful has created a passion in our hearts, we can be certain the resources are reserved in heaven to equip us to get the job done. Ask Him for them. He wants His heavenly host to join with His Church to do the work.

He will be glorified as we hold on until we receive the promise. And He will be glorified in blessing us.

*For it is God which worketh in you both to will*
*and to do of his good pleasure.*
*– Philippians 2:13*

*For the LORD God is a sun and shield;*
*The LORD will give grace and glory;*
*No good thing will He withhold*
*From those who walk uprightly.*
*– Psalm 84:11*

# EMBRACED

*"His left hand is under my head."*
– SONG OF SOLOMON 2:6

*"The Lord gives his beloved sleep."*
– PSALM 127:2

In rest the Lord is gently cradling our heads. He would let no harm come to us, ever watchful, ever vigilant, ever mindful of our safety and refreshing. He is security, and *"underneath are the everlasting arms."* Deuteronomy 33:27

Fall into His safety net. Trust him. He is more than able. Lean on Him. He is more than sure. He does not disappoint but leads us safely through the night.

*"His right arm embraces me."*
– SONG OF SOLOMON 8:3

Ready to go, upright, mobilized, called to action, the Lord holds us up and guides us. His powerful right arm guides and moves us forward. He is our strong fortress. In His arms there is joy. He is our strength forever more. In Him there is a sure future. From His high tower we can see.

Only in His arms can we sidestep disaster. We must let Him lead. He is Lord of the dance.

*My beloved is mine, and I am his.*
*He feeds his flock among the lilies.*

*Until the day breaks and the shadows flee away,*
*Turn, my beloved, and be like a gazelle*
*Or a young stag upon the mountains of Bether.*
– SONG OF SOLOMON 2:16–17

# STAND STILL

Sometimes all we are asked to do is to *stand* with our full armor on and our swords sharpened. It does not successfully advance the kingdom of God to go out before He orders us to do so. We need to be individually and corporately waiting on Him. We must do all He is asking us to do, but not more. If we are to be waiting for orders to advance and step out of the protection of doing just that, we open ourselves up to conflict we are ill equipped to win.

> *Therefore the prudent keep silent at that time,*
> *For it is an evil time.*
> – AMOS 5:13

This silence is something to ponder. There is a time to be still. Perhaps to wait and be strengthened. Should we feverishly intercede during this time? Or labor desperately over lost souls? Do not be caught in the trap of commanding an army of one. We are in this as servants, not commanders. It is not our battle but the Lord's.

The devil will taunt and stir up trouble for all he is worth. He wants to defeat us before he himself is defeated. We are desperate for an example of rest, peace, courage, and confident determination in the midst of his devilish pranks. Let us look to Jesus! What determination! What peace!

His eyes were fixed on the "Joy set before him." He neither waivered to the right nor to the left, but the straight, narrow beam the Father had laid out for Him. The devil will distract us, sideswipe us, even with a full frontal attack, but though he did all of this and more to Jesus, He never wavered.

The Holy Spirit was sent from heaven to those who believe that He might witness to us of Jesus. He works in us to make us like Jesus, so that He can work through us. Our efforts will not give us victory. We depend on Him for everything. So *wait* on Him. He will yet prove Himself victorious if we belong to Him and are willing to let Him be Lord.

*So he answered and said to me:*
*This is the word of the LORD to Zerubbabel:*
*'Not by might nor by power, but by My Spirit,'*
*Says the LORD of hosts.*
*– ZECHARIAH 4:6*

# BATTLE-WORN

Battle-worn
Shell-shocked
Mocked
Torn

Your church
Your sheep
Scattered
Forlorn

The Good Shepherd
Gathers
In loving arms

The wounded
The tattered
The scattered
The torn

Come!

Rest ye weary
Repent ye wayward
Be healed ye wounded
Be bound ye torn

The Father
Is waiting
Good pleasure
To perform

Take your seats
All ye tried
Fill your plates
All ye torn

The invitations sent
The banquet prepared
Fill your plates ye weary
Imbibe deeply ye torn

The table is set
In the midst of your foes
Eat hearty my children
Drink lusty my torn

*You prepare a table before me in the presence of my enemies;*
*You anoint my head with oil; my cup runs over.*
*– PSALM 23:5*

# Until the Day Breaks

The sun is full and the sky is so blue. Spring is peeking through the curtains of winter with promise of new life.

There is fog, however, covering the mountain of my mind. Something sparkles in it but I can't yet discern what. Here a thought and there a thought ... like puzzle pieces under gauze.

*"Awake o North wind, and come O South! Blow upon*
*my garden, that its spices may flow out...."*
— Song of Songs 4: 16a.

*Until the day breaks*
*And the shadows flee away,*
*I will go my way to the mountain of myrrh*
*And to the hill of frankincense.*
— Song of Songs 4:6

# Fear Not

*But we have this treasure in earthen vessels, that the excellence of
the power may be of God and not of us. We are hard-pressed on
every side, yet not crushed; we are perplexed, but not in despair;
persecuted, but not forsaken; struck down, but not destroyed.*

*– 2 Corinthians 4:7–9*

God created man in His image and likeness and said His creation was
very good. Like God, we are emotional beings. Unlike God, our
emotions are no longer pure and sinless. Although there are many times
when we, as the Redeemed, know our emotions are in harmony with
God, Satan fights for control in this area of our lives.

We are in the time of a "face off" for the lordship of our emotions.
Fear, panic, rage, hatred, confusion, despair, rebellion, depression, loneliness, guilt, pride, and the list could go on and on.

Enter the twenty-first-century battleground raging in the spirit world
for the hearts and souls of men.

Terrorism is not in the Devil's arsenal by mistake. He wants prisoners
in the grip of fear, using it to entangle and enslave us to the wrong master.
Fear has a death grip if ever there was one. It is powerful and binding.

We long for security. If we yield to the ways of the world to obtain it,
we are setting our feet on shifting, unstable sand. There is no comfort or
rest in being off balance.

We grab at straws
That are already
Set on fire.

78

*These things I have spoken to you, that in Me you may have peace.*
*In the world you will have tribulation; but be of good cheer,*
*I have overcome the world.*

*– JOHN 16:33*

How often does God's Word tell us not to fear? He knew we desperately need to hear it. We need to hear the voice of our King as He comforts us and assures us of His control. "Do not fear," says the tender Shepherd to the sheep, "I have overcome the world. I am Conquering King. Indeed, I have already claimed victory for you."

God has a redemption plan for our whole being, not just part. We are told in Scripture to renew our minds. It is a way to victory over the sinful paths to which our nature leans.

Once we realize that our minds need renewing, we begin to understand that renewal must not stop there. WE need renewing. ALL of us, no portion left behind, emotional responses included.

Emotions don't always cooperate. Sometimes we are so compelled by their grip we act out according to the way we feel without even knowing we are doing it, much less knowing how to stop. They can be so strong they overpower our ability to hear the Holy Spirit's whisper. His voice is the one we all want to hear and obey.

We must let the words of our Savior wash over us.

Can you hear Him say…

*There is no fear in love; but perfect love casts out fear,*
*because fear involves torment. But he who fears has not been*
*made perfect in love. We love Him because He first loved us.*

*– 1 JOHN 4:18–19*

*For whatever is born of God overcomes the world.*
*And this is the victory that has overcome the world—our faith.*

*– 1 JOHN 5:4*

*Therefore, since a promise remains of entering His rest,*
*let us fear lest any of you seem to have come short of it.*
*– HEBREWS 4:1*

*For God has not given us a spirit of fear,*
*but of power and of love and of a sound mind.*
*– 2 TIMOTHY 1:7*

*Teaching them to observe all things that I have commanded you;*
*and lo, I am with you always, even to the end of the age. Amen.*
*– MATTHEW 28:20*

Take courage, beloved of the Father!

*"Do not fear, little flock, for it is your Father's good*
*pleasure to give you the kingdom."*
*– LUKE 12:32*

# SEEK THE BEST

If we ever prayed that the Lord would give us understanding, knowledge or wisdom, we are sure to get our requests for we pray according to His will. He says seek earnestly the best gifts. How hot is the fire and how deep are the waters we are willing to go through?

> *But earnestly desire the best gifts.*
> – 1 CORINTHIANS 12:31

If we find ourselves spun out of control in the storm of anger, the deepest darkest cave of depression, or the crowded cities of loneliness, we can know that God is working something redemptive in us.

The Holy Spirit does not always take us on the easy route of safety and comfort. He takes our hand and leads instead through a world of danger. Any child of God can see the evil of the fallen world.

If we retreat in the face of evil, let us remember to retreat into the merciful arms of the Living God. It is not wrong to retreat into His arms. There the weary find refreshing, Listen for His voice. Is He calling you forward? Is He calling you down, down into the bedrock of His arms?

If we dig in with Him, embracing Him in the midst of the overwhelming ocean that captures us, we will hit bedrock. There is an end where we will meet the sure foundation. There we will be trampolined into higher freedom in the truth of who He is in us.

> *"Fear not, for I have redeemed you;*
> *I have called you by your name;*
> *You are Mine.*
> *When you pass through the waters, I will be with you;*

*And through the rivers, they shall not overflow you.*
*When you walk through the fire, you shall not be burned,*
*Nor shall the flame scorch you.*
*For I am the LORD your God,*
*The Holy One of Israel, your Savior;*

– ISAIAH 43:1B–3A

# THROUGH

As I walk through a door, or perhaps a tunnel, leading to physical healing these past months, I realize that there is a battle raging to keep me from walking in the healed body God has for me. As I was pondering this journey, wondering which evil principality or power afflicted me with such physical wounding, the word "dominion" settled in my thinking.

In *Webster's New Universal Unabridged Dictionary*, the word "dominion" is explained in part as "power or right of governing and controlling, sovereign authority," and "a territory usually of considerable size in which a single rulership holds sway." The current ruler need not be the legitimate one. He just remains in primary control until there is a ground swell of revolt and his lordship is given to another.

I am holding on to the Lord who has the legal right to me, the title deed to this domain. Even if the other is not convinced, I know he is not the ruler over the structure of my body. Many scrimmages have been won on my behalf in the area of illness. Sicknesses of many kinds have been diminished in strength or roundly defeated. God has done the routing. I have walked in healthy thanksgiving.

This current difficulty He is taking me through seems to be on a different battlefield. It is resistant and strong, and it cripples me over and over even where there is no apparent foothold. There has been discouragement, impatience, pain, setbacks, isolation, inability, tension, sleeplessness, weariness, fatigue, and on and on. There are many adversaries.

Fortunately, there is a place called Through, and it is where I am going. I am on a journey beyond this dark place, to His kingdom where all is subject to His rule. I am not willing to let go of His hand until I have arrived. I am a child of God. For a long part of the trip, I intend to be holding His hand, skipping along. For some miles He may be dragging me, but I will not let go.

> *Then Jesus, being filled with the Holy Spirit, returned from the Jordan and was led by the Spirit into the wilderness, being tempted for forty days by the devil. And in those days, He ate nothing, and afterward, when they had ended, He was hungry.*
> – LUKE 4:1–2

> *Then Jesus returned in the power of the Spirit to Galilee, and news of Him went out through all the surrounding region.*
> – LUKE 4:14

# I Am a Dead Man

I am a dead man.
How can the bulls of Bashan hurt me?
Though their threats and
Snorting smoke engulf me and
Their roaring fills my ears
The Lord and His peace are
Within
Greater than that which is
Without
Oh Lord, make haste to help me
Deliver your darling from the
Crushing noise of pain
You surround me with
Loving kindness and the
Tenderest of mercies
Melody and
Nourishment come
To my door
The incense of the saints
Ascends to the throne of
Mercy and grace.
Stability and confidence in
Cool refreshing waves
Follow the
Tears of my groaning
Who would not call this rich?
Your close friendship and

Sovereign lordship
Make me rich!
All my swollen needs
Attended to by You
Blow upon my battered frame
Hold fast my name
I love
How
You love me

*I have been crucified with Christ; it is no longer I who live,*
*but Christ lives in me; and the life which I now live in the flesh*
*I live by faith in the Son of God, who loved me and*
*gave Himself for me.*
*– GALATIANS 2:20*

# A Moment with You

We are in troubled waters
Roaring distractions block our view
Raging details demand our attention
We long for the languid

Walk away for a moment to gaze
On Your beauty
Wait on the Lord and He shall give you
The desires
Of your heart

After a moment with You
The waters are more peaceful
Distractions subdued
Details settled

Return once more for a long, deep drink

Leave my heart on gentle simmer
And the duties of the day be done
To Your glory
In Your strength
In lingering power of time spent wisely
If briefly
In the stillness of Your beauty

*And let the beauty of the LORD our God be upon us,*
*And establish the work of our hands for us;*
*Yes, establish the work of our hands.*
*– PSALM 90:17*

# OLD SKIN

A time of shedding old wineskin to make a worthy vessel for new wine requires a depth of physical "slaying." I rise up from the path of self-sufficiency to find a greater, not lesser, need to be crucified with Christ moment by furious moment as the details of life move in with renewed intensity. Self dies hard.

O Holy God! Who can win this battle? That which I would NOT, that I do! That which I would, that I do not! Who can save me from this wickedness?! Thanks be to God I have found a Savior! Nothing is too hard for Him.

> Then the disciples of John came to Him, saying, "Why do we and the Pharisees fast often, but Your disciples do not fast?" And Jesus said to them, "Can the friends of the bridegroom mourn as long as the bridegroom is with them? But the days will come when the bridegroom will be taken away from them, and then they will fast. No one puts a piece of unshrunk cloth on an old garment; for the patch pulls away from the garment, and the tear is made worse. Nor do they put new wine into old wineskins, or else the wineskins break, the wine is spilled, and the wineskins are ruined. But they put new wine into new wineskins, and both are preserved."
>
> – MATTHEW 9:14–17

> He must increase, but I must decrease.
>
> – JOHN 3:30

# RELATIONSHIPS

Relationships left dragging at such a distance, how can they be called such? Communication left to die of neglect, how can it be renewed?

Let go the rope or
Breathe new life into the vine
It is way too big a thing for me
It is a small matter for You

You walk before me into Galilee
All my tomorrows
Moment by moment
Pass through Your fingers

Though I see no life
Yet there is life
For all my paths
Are in You

Breathe, Spirit of Life
Into the cord that binds us together

*And everyone who has left houses or brothers or sisters or father*
*or mother or wife*[a] *or children or lands, for My name's sake, shall*
*receive a hundredfold, and inherit eternal life.*
*– Matthew 19:29*

# JUST BECAUSE

Just because He wants to bless me
He wants to bless me just because
To bless me just because He wants to
Just because
He does

Time and again I have come for blessing with eyes unable to see, needy and despairing, only to be overtaken with grace, overcome with the astonishing flow of His goodwill toward me.

How great is our God! How great His goodness! His blessings reach to the darkest places of any needy heart. His mercy! His grace! His pure benevolence to the low. Such tenderness and generosity radiating from Him, extending to find a resting place in my receiving heart.

*Take what is yours and go your way. I wish to give*
*to this last man the same as to you.*
*– MATTHEW 20:14*

# Hope Splattered

*When they had crossed over, they came to the land of Gennesaret.*
*And when the men of that place recognized Him, they sent out*
*into all that surrounding region, brought to Him all who were*
*sick, and begged Him that they might only touch the hem of His*
*garment. And as many as touched it were made perfectly well.*
*– Matthew 14:34–36*

Is not the real Jesus here?
The same as in the Scripture above?
The One moved with compassion
Mercy and love?
Were not all healed by a mere
Touch of His hem?
And I hang on and cling!
Does faith waiver?
Is hope spattered in tears
On the ground?
Yes, it does. Yes, it is.

I will lift up my eyes
From whence cometh thy glory!? (help)
The Lord Strong and Mighty!
The Lord mighty in battle.
He is the King of Glory!
Let the King of Glory come in!
The Lord Strong and Mighty in battle!
The battle belongs to the Lord!

Little ones to Him belong,
It is good to be weak!
He will show HIMSELF strong.

In Your glory I am undone.
At Your hem is where I belong.

*And suddenly, a woman who had a flow of blood for twelve years came from behind and touched the hem of His garment.* [21] *For she said to herself, "If only I may touch His garment, I shall be made well."* [22] *But Jesus turned around, and when He saw her He said, "Be of good cheer, daughter; your faith has made you well." And the woman was made well from that hour.*

– MATTHEW 9:20–22

# STOPPED TO RELEASE

How can it possibly be
God's will for me to be stopped by pain?
If He is sovereign then this too is His will
He will work all together
Mixing mashing fitting it
For good
His good
My good
'Til I be formed complete in Him
Transformed complete for Him
My good
His good
Mashed and mixed
A life for Him
His pleasure
My delight
In Him

A mystery to be sure
So hard to let go of selfish ambition

*Yes, and all who desire to live godly in Christ Jesus*
*will suffer persecution.*
*– 2 TIMOTHY 3:12*

# CHILD'S BAD DAY

Crabby, irritable, fussy
Hovering and protective
He comes
Discontent, myopic, restless
Loving and languid
He comes
Fearful, pensive, uncertain
Clear and unfeigning
He comes
Roaming, wandering, defensive
Steady and accepting
He comes

When a child has a bad night, or a bad day, or a bad stretch of days, a papa's heart searches the depths in patient love 'til the chord of truth is strummed and peaceful harmony returns, restored. Patient waiting, ceaseless loving, pure acceptance is a threefold cord not easily broken or escaped even though there be immaturity and rebellion battling for the soul.

To Thine own name
Be true
Abba Father
I love how You love me!

*My Father, who has given them to Me, is greater than all; and no one is able to snatch them out of My Father's hand.*
*– JOHN 10:29*

# COAL WITH A GLOW

Six feet under, lying in state
Pushing up daisies, that is our fate
Rules and regulations, ordinance of man
Seeking resolution in the worldly plan
What will it get you? Results are the same
Every road leads to the end of the game

Bow low in obedience, submit to the Cross
All the world said was gain is just murky dross
Good health is an asset in the world's employ
Dead men do not need it to walk
In love and peace and joy

Unless we embrace the Savior of the Cross
All we thought was gain, we'll count as filthy loss
Six feet under, lying in state
Pushing up daisies, that is our fate

*For as many as are of the works of the law are under the curse;*
*for it is written, "Cursed is everyone who does not continue in all*
*things which are written in the book of the law, to do them."*
*– GALATIANS 3:10*

# RESTORED TO FAITH

I'm ready oh so ready
To shout Your praises Lord
Help from man is futile
Only God can help me
Only in Him do I
Find my answers

Hope in man's knowledge, learning and skill has left me where I
started. There is always one more thing to try, one more road to
explore in my search for physical health, one more piece of advice to fol-
low. "This" doesn't bring relief, so try "that."

This morning's reading of Psalm 108 again reminds me that God
alone is my solution, that He loves me so much.

He will hear my cry because of who He is. If one reason isn't enough,
the second is His tenderness toward a needy child, whom He loves.

He is:

Provider – sacred abundance
Papa – carrier of concern
Healer – gentle fixer
Truth – unfailing standard

The steadiness of my wait is restored
But more
I rise up to test the extent
Of today's provision
I don't want to waste it
By lack of use

*Be exalted, O God, above the heavens,*
*And Your glory above all the earth;*
*That Your beloved may be delivered,*
*Save with Your right hand, and hear me.*
*– PSALM 108:5–6*


*Give us help from trouble,*
*For the help of man is useless.*
*¹³ Through God we will do valiantly,*
*For it is He who shall tread down our enemies.*
*– PSALM 108:12–13*

# Mercy in the Flames

Let the fire burn my dross consume
Be merciful in Thy flaming love my Lord
Until refining fire hath its purpose won
In the midst of the flame
Though hot and sore
There is comfort for the one whose hope is the Lord

*Create in me a clean heart oh Lord*
*And renew a right Spirit in me*
*Cast me not away from thy presence*
*Restore to me the joy of my salvation*

*– PSALM 51:10–11*

*Let patience have its perfect work.*

*– JAMES 1:4*

# PERFECTION MY TARGET

The target is perfection. Jesus is the perfect one. Aiming at any other target is to aim amiss and we will surely not attain the purity and perfection that our hearts long for. The pathway of holiness leads to Him who is holy.

> *Therefore gird up the loins of your mind, be sober, and rest your*
> *hope fully upon the grace that is to be brought to you at the*
> *revelation of Jesus Christ; as obedient children, not conforming*
> *yourselves to the former lusts, as in your ignorance; but as*
> *He who called you is holy, you also be holy in all your conduct,*
> *because it is written, "Be holy, for I am holy."*
> – 1 PETER 1:13–16

Jesus has walked humanity's arduous path. His footsteps always led to the Father. How can we more closely follow Jesus on this carefully selected road?

Romans Chapter 12 gives a snapshot of a life well lived in Christ. It does not necessarily describe the specific duty of the day, for we all have different functions in the body of believers, but the wholehearted expenditure of ourselves in service as the Lord works through us His good pleasure.

We present our bodies as a living sacrifice. It is by the mercies of God we are beseeched to do so, and by the very mercies of God that we present. In and of ourselves, there is no good thing. Go ahead and try in your own self to prove what is good and acceptable before God. Every time it will end up in self-aggrandizement, doing in your own strength, proving yourself. And even while proving that which is good in yourself, the arrow is aimed at imperfection and falls short of the glory God has planned for us.

We pick and choose along the way, doing impulsively or planning carefully, activities, good works, or services of every kind that He has chosen to place before us. More than what we do, however, is the attitude of our hearts in the life we live moment by moment and day by challenging day.

Oh, there is imperfect wreckage in the wake of my life. The cross of Christ that I share with my dear Lord has room enough for all of it. Huge chunks of self- ambition, self-promotion, self-exalting motives, self-satisfaction, self-pleasures and self-defense lie as an apron of burnt flesh over the yoke in which I am coupled with a meek, gentle, humble Savior.

> *I have been crucified with Christ; it is no longer I who live, but*
> *Christ lives in me; and the life which I now live in the flesh*
> *I live by faith in the Son of God,*
> *who loved me and gave Himself for me.*
> – GALATIANS 2:20

The degree of glory God has planned for us, working in us and through us, will be aimed at the perfect person of Jesus, to make us like Him. We cannot miss if daily we take up our cross and present ourselves as living sacrifices.

Jesus promises that in taking up His yoke we find our rest. Self-service, self-perfecting, self-promoting weariness dies as we join with Him on the cross.

> Submitted unto this cross of perfection
> Yielded and obedient to the yoke
> I find liberty
> Only in surrender

Do I find true freedom
For His yoke is easy
And His burden is light

*I beseech you therefore, brethren, by the mercies of God,
that you present your bodies a living sacrifice, holy, acceptable
to God, which is your reasonable service. And do not be
conformed to this world, but be transformed by the renewing
of your mind, that you may prove what is that good and
acceptable and perfect will of God.*

*– ROMANS 12:1–2*

# You Are

Lord
You are
My source and my supply
My frame and my form
My fuel and my fire
My core and my crown

*I have been crucified with Christ; it is no longer I who live, but*
*Christ lives in me; and the life which I now live in the flesh*
*I live by faith in the Son of God,*
*who loved me and gave Himself for me.*

*– GALATIANS 2:20*

# He Cares

When I am at the deepest, darkest point in life, God is there. When I am struggling in pain, can't pray, can't think, God is there. When my life comes to a halt and all that ever helped to define me and give my life meaning ceases, God is there.

God cares. He hears the pain of my body cry out to Him. He sees the scattered pieces of my mind as I search for meaning, for value, for purpose, for comfort. He comes. When I can bear it no longer, He holds me still. He turns my sweating struggle into harnessed hope.

When my identity is shattered, God is there.

He cares.

He knows my name.

> *Where can I go from Your Spirit?*
> *Or where can I flee from Your presence?*
> *If I ascend into heaven, You are there;*
> *If I make my bed in hell, behold, You are there.*
> *If I take the wings of the morning,*
> *And dwell in the uttermost parts of the sea,*
> *Even there Your hand shall lead me,*
> *And Your right hand shall hold me.*
>
> – Psalm 139:7–10

# He Delivers

After having tasted the goodness of God, it is impossible not to want more. There is a banquet set before me in the presence of my enemies!

The surpassing wonder of that kingdom-come wedding feast He is preparing is beginning to make me ravenous for Him. I do believe He has been dishing out taste tests of the good things He has prepared for those who love Him. He lingers over each item, seasoning and stirring, simmering and tasting, and lets us taste a morsel of this future banquet! It is good! It is good!! It is good!!!

I pray that this prep time is spent adding final touches to the delicious and fulfilling blessings He has for us, and I also pray that He expands our capacity to handle the scrumptious meal He is preparing.

I'd like to drive a great big semitruck to the catering hall, back it up, load it full of samples and deliver them to all His called and chosen.

Ooooh! That would be fun!

*You prepare a table before me in the presence of my enemies;*
*You anoint my head with oil; my cup runs over.*

*– Psalm 23:5*

# Prayer Army

Roadway of mercy
Pathway of joy
Quick to enlist
Fast to deploy
God's marching army
Flies to the scene
Tenderly touching
The meek and the mean

Transforming power
Flows from His throne
Gentling danger
Befriending alone
Filling the spaces
Left vacant 'til now
Sinner made saint
Crowning His brow

*The Lord gave the word; great was the company*
*of those who proclaimed it.*
*– Psalm 68:11*

# I Am a Stump

Is it all right to be a stump
When trees surrounding are in bloom
When willows dance and pines stand tall

Is it okay to be a stump?

Is it all right to be a stump
When fruit trees bear abundant juice
And yellow birds fill the thickets

Is it okay to be a stump?

Is it okay to be a stump
When muscled oaks stretch and bend
When chattering aspens fill the air

Is it all right?

Come, weary one
Rest
For you, I am a stump

*For we dare not class ourselves or compare ourselves with those*
*who commend themselves. But they, measuring themselves*
*by themselves, and comparing themselves among themselves,*
*are not wise.*
*– 2 Corinthians 10:12*

# LIFE'S MOMENTUM

Open your bible and follow along in Proverbs 31:10–27. My bible tells me that these verses are an acrostic, each verse beginning with a successive letter of the Hebrew alphabet. It occurred to me that it is also a progression of a married woman's life in Christ.

Vs. 11–12, He finds a woman he can safely trust. She is determined to stand by him and do what is right. He falls in love determined to encourage this standard in her and tries to live up to it himself. She brings him good … he lacks nothing of value. I love that. The value here has nothing to do with material wealth; that comes later. This value is beyond earthly riches. Integrity, honesty, perseverance, faithfulness, and stability are a few of those riches.

Continuing in vs. 13–14, she eagerly fills her hand with things to do and accumulates, with thoughts of what to do later. She is seeking the material now that will service her household later. She researches. Where are the best vendors to find material for clothing and food? Durable goods, furniture—she sets up her household. These are important things, for by vs.15 she no longer has time to do that kind of shopping. Now a child has been born and she is rising while it is still dark and providing food for her family.

Who of us mothers managed to wriggle out of every nighttime feeding and have our husbands do them? Maybe an occasional one. But most were provided by Mom. Who of us rose and told the baby to go back to sleep because it wasn't yet morning? I tried that a time or two but it didn't work. Babies demand faithfulness.

She also, during this time, plans for and influences a servant girl. Today the babysitter definitely fits that role. Mom needs to go out and during that time she has her household in order, so the sitter doesn't lose her mind while she watches the kids! She provides all her "servant girl" needs to make the job successful. She is faithful to give bread in keeping with the task. She pays the going rate, and sometimes extra.

Vs. 16, 17, 18. She considers a field. This seems to speak of a wonderful training ground for her children. A vineyard is mentioned in scripture, perhaps a recycling business today or any number of creative things a family can do together. This has a twofold purpose: to help support the family and make it prosper, and to provide training for the growing children.

The initial effort requires a lot of hard work up front. Do not make light of the words she considers. This requires prayer, planning, research, and vision. But when she is satisfied that it will work for a teaching ground and a benefit, she digs in.

She is the hardworking startup person who gets the ball rolling, works to be an example, and then teaches her children to pitch in.

Vs. 18b. Her lamp does not go out at night. She does not give up when the going gets tough. She sees the investment as profitable and helpful to establish those family values in every member of her household. She remains invested.

That often requires extra prayer after the household goes to bed for the night. This is time for intercession and personal growth, not to mention paperwork and paying bills!

Vs. 19 and 20. Here, at an older age, her children are doing most of the household chores. They have learned to invest themselves in "the family business" and have even become responsible for it. She has the oversight. She keeps busy, however, so as not to hover. She trusts but keeps a watchful eye. Needlework keeps her busy but she can remain somewhat engaged and so do many other of the hobbies and passions in which women love to participate. Her age demands a different level of activity, but this stage opens up wonderful volunteer opportunities. She now has not only time but also resources of accumulated knowledge and material goods to offer.

The Lord has prospered her. Her faithfulness, perseverance, and hard work have been rewarded, and the next stage in life has a promise of fullness and abundance in it.

Vs. 21. When it snows, she looks to the future and has confidence for all her family. She is not afraid of old age.

She is stable and secure. The good effort she has put into parenting will continue in the next generations.

Vs. 22. Bed coverings and clothed in linen and purple. Her children and all who know her have in some way been blessed by her. Her children are of noble character and are ready to be prayerfully launched into productive independent lives.

Vs. 23. Her husband holds his head high. All her blessings belong to him. He has chosen well. She has been an undergirding for him. Because of this, he is lifted up and held in honor and respect by those who know, deal with, and speak about him. All the faithful give him a good review. She has joined him in earning it.

Vs. 24. She sells and she sends. She becomes a merchant herself for those who need one. She sends forth her productive, bill-paying children to establish their own homes, benefiting the merchants and making "fat their sashes."

Vs. 25. There is such grace about this woman, such confidence, such security and inner strength. She can laugh! Not simply smile but laugh. There is no weapon that can prosper against her, and she knows it.

Vs. 26 and 27. Instructing grandchildren and young mothers is the next natural stage, and she is able to fill the need with love and understanding. She is vigilant to battle in prayer. Though her body does not have the vigor of youth, she, in her more sedentary life, is far from lazy or inactive. She remains caring, compassionate, and refrains from the temptation to gossip. Her prayer life does not coast in idleness but shifts to rise to the top of the hills and the depth of the valleys her children and grandchildren face, with power, patience, confidence, and success. She has become a steadfast warrior and remains faithful in oversight.

The works of her husband and children provide a lasting legacy of honor and praise. The entire city benefits from her faithful service to God.

Her children rise up and call her blessed;
Her husband also, and he praises her:
"Many daughters have done well,
But you excel them all."
Charm is deceitful and beauty is passing,
But a woman who fears the LORD, she shall be praised.
Give her of the fruit of her hands,
And let her own works praise her in the gates.
– PROVERBS 31:28-31

# Achoo!

*When Elisha came into the house, there was the child, lying dead*
*on his bed. He went in therefore, shut the door behind the two of*
*them, and prayed to the LORD. And he went up and lay on the*
*child, and put his mouth on his mouth, his eyes on his eyes, and*
*his hands on his hands; and he stretched himself out on the child,*
*and the flesh of the child became warm. He returned and walked*
*back and forth in the house, and again went up and stretched*
*himself out on him; then the child sneezed seven times, and the*
*child opened his eyes. And he called Gehazi and said, "Call this*
*Shunammite woman." So he called her. And when she came in to*
*him, he said, "Pick up your son."*
*– 2 KINGS 4:32–36*

Recently, there was a thought clinging to me about sneezing—and this
story about Elisha came to mind.

"Sneeze" in the Hebrew also means "to diffuse." I believe the Lord
is gathering us corporately and privately, lying on us (and sometimes I
think He has been lying on us to keep us from moving!), and breathing
life into us. When He has accomplished the full extent of His task, we
individually and corporately will "sneeze" or burst or diffuse His life like
never before. I would so love to be a part of a seven-sneeze event! What
fun! What glory!

*But you shall receive power when the Holy Spirit has come upon*
*you; and you shall be witnesses to Me in Jerusalem, and in all*
*Judea and Samaria, and to the end of the earth.*
*– ACTS 1:8*

# EVER NEARER

More and more I am hearing talk about the unity of the church and the coming of that unity and the incredible power of it. I can easily believe it. We are stepping ever closer to being one holy and spotless Bride, receiving from the Lord and moving in the power of the Spirit in perfect harmony. The momentum and power of it will be unstoppable and awesome to behold.

The energy of one walking with the Lord is greatly to be desired. The synergy of many doing the same obedient walk will be a force unhindered and full of glory. Indeed, His power requires many vessels to flow through. It is my heart's desire to see it, and I pray to be a part of it.

Know Him. Be reserved for that time when your slot in the force opens up. Then move in step and fill it.

It is a message worth shouting from the rooftops.

> *But you are a chosen generation, a royal priesthood, a holy*
> *nation, His own special people, that you may proclaim the praises*
> *of Him who called you out of darkness into His marvelous light;*
> *– 1 PETER 2:9*

> *Then Jesus answered and said to them,*
> *"Most assuredly,*
> *I say to you, the Son can do nothing of Himself,*
> *but what He sees the Father do;*
> *for whatever He does*
> *the Son also does in like manner.*
> *– JOHN 5:19*

# HIS TENDER
# LISTENING EAR

Sometimes I think of Father in human terms and think He must get sick of my tears and heart cries. Then I remember that He is not that way.

That every time I come is new and fresh to Him.
That He is ripening this heart for His own good pleasure, and in His own carefully designed timing.
That my tears are precious to Him—so much so that He saves each one.
That this heart cry, in words that cannot be uttered—is a work of His very own Spirit abiding in me.
That I am not alone and am joining others to fill up the attic of incense, until it satisfies Father's heart.
That His ear is ever attentive.
That He searches for those who worship in spirit and truth.
That He runs to the rescue of the needy.
That the blood of His Perfect Son covers me and makes me a pure delight to Him.

What confidence I have in approaching His tender listening ear. So often I have few requests that I can understand. Mostly just deep ache and longing need, infused with such love and such gratitude that I weep. He is so unlike any person I have ever known.

He does not grow weary.
His mercies are new every morning.
He changes not.
Great is His Faithfulness.

*You number my wanderings;*
*Put my tears into Your bottle;*
*Are they not in Your book?*
*– PSALM 56:8*

*Likewise the Spirit also helps in our weaknesses. For we do not*
*know what we should pray for as we ought, but the Spirit Himself*
*makes intercession for us with groanings which cannot be uttered.*
*– ROMANS 8:26*

*And the smoke of the incense, with the prayers of the saints,*
*ascended before God from the angel's hand.*
*– REVELATIONS 8:4*

# BELOVED

Purity of heart
Singleness of vision
Angles of hope
Love power driven

Coiffed hair and down
Chin lifted high
Galleries enclosed
Broad as the sky

Mute before men
World in a pen

Cherished and pure
Strongly demure

Enclosed
Set free
Reposed
'Neath tree

*My heart is overflowing with a good theme;*
*I recite my composition concerning the King;*
*My tongue is the pen of a ready writer.*

*– PSALM 45:1*

# ENGRAVED ON THE
# STATUE OF LIBERTY

"Give me your tired
Your poor
Your huddled masses
Yearning to breathe free
The wretched refuse
Of your teeming shore

Send these the homeless
The tempest-tossed
To me

I lift my lamp
Beside the
Golden door"

Could we as a church dare to stand beside the
golden door and lift high the lamp of God
for the teeming masses to see?
OH!
Dare we?
Please, dare we!

*The people who walked in darkness*
*Have seen a great light;*
*Those who dwelt in the land of the shadow of death,*
*Upon them a light has shined.*
*– ISAIAH 9:2*

# EMPTY WITH A PURPOSE

It is good to be empty with a purpose.

*A certain woman of the wives of the sons of the prophets cried out to Elisha, saying, "Your servant my husband is dead, and you know that your servant feared the LORD. And the creditor is coming to take my two sons to be his slaves." So Elisha said to her, "What shall I do for you? Tell me, what do you have in the house?" And she said, "Your maidservant has nothing in the house but a jar of oil." Then he said, "Go, borrow vessels from everywhere, from all your neighbors—empty vessels; do not gather just a few. And when you have come in, you shall shut the door behind you and your sons; then pour it into all those vessels, and set aside the full ones." So she went from him and shut the door behind her and her sons, who brought the vessels to her; and she poured it out. Now it came to pass, when the vessels were full, that she said to her son, "Bring me another vessel." And he said to her, "There is not another vessel." So the oil ceased. Then she came and told the man of God. And he said, "Go, sell the oil and pay your debt; and you and your sons live on the rest."*

*– 2 KINGS 4:1–7*

# DRAWN OUT

As I was contemplating where Holy Spirit might lead me, I found myself in Zachariah Chapter 4.

*So he answered and said to me:*
*"This is the word of the LORD to Zerubbabel:*
*'Not by might nor by power, but by My Spirit,'*
*Says the LORD of hosts.*
*– ZACHARIAH 4:6*

The basic meaning of Zerubbabel is "drawn out of Babylon." As the Church, the Bride, is drawn out of this world system and separated unto the Lord, I am seeing His Holy Spirit consistently doing wonders, small wonders that my eyes have been opened by Him to see.

Who despises the day of small things? Not I!

How mighty in His hand we will become. We will begin the work and see its end. The capstone will be brought out with shouts of Grace! Grace to it!

Oh, the wondrous joy of This My God!

*"Who are you, O great mountain?*
*Before Zerubbabel you shall become a plain!*
*And he shall bring forth the capstone*
*With shouts of 'Grace, grace to it!'*
*For who has despised the day of small things?*
*For these seven rejoice to see*
*The plumb line in the hand of Zerubbabel.*
*They are the eyes of the LORD,*
*Which scan to and fro throughout the whole earth."*
*– ZACHARIAH 4:7,10*

# BUMBLE BEE

God wants a people who will "bee" for Him
It doesn't matter your abilities, just be
A lesson from the bumblebee, a very humblebee
Makes no sense that he can fly
But when God gives him the job
Of gathering pollen
Off he flies
He's all abuzz
He just obeys
It's what he does!
God wants some bees!
Come on! Let's buzz!

*But to each one of us grace was given according*
*to the measure of Christ's gift. Therefore He says:*
*"When He ascended on high,*
*He led captivity captive,*
*And gave gifts to men."*

*– EPHESIANS 4:7–8*

# HE IS MY
# RIGHTEOUSNESS

2 Samuel Chapter 22 caught my eye today. I couldn't get beyond the first lines before I melted in a puddle of tears before Him.

*And he said:*
*"The LORD is my rock and my fortress and my deliverer;*
*The God of my strength, in whom I will trust;*
*My shield and the horn of my salvation,*
*My stronghold and my refuge;*
*My Savior, You save me from violence.*
*I will call upon the LORD, who is worthy to be praised;*
*So shall I be saved from my enemies.*
*– 2 SAMUEL 22:2–4*

David's song of praise rings in my heart as my very own. But as I recovered and continued reading, the ownership grew stronger.

One of the most clinging and intriguing passages begins in vs. 21.

*"The LORD rewarded me according to my righteousness;*
*According to the cleanness of my hands*
*He has recompensed me.*
*For I have kept the ways of the LORD,*
*And have not wickedly departed from my God.*
*– 2 SAMUEL 22:21–22*

Having entered into Him who is my righteousness, I am clothed about with His righteousness. However, the Lord looks down to see my behavior and my actions confirm my position in Him. What I do speaks to Him. What I do speaks to me. Obedience to God produces in me the boldness and confidence I need to confront my enemies.

*"I have pursued my enemies and destroyed them;*
*Neither did I turn back again till they were destroyed.*
*And I have destroyed them and wounded them,*
*So that they could not rise;*
*They have fallen under my feet.*
*– 2 Samuel 22:38-39*

Oh! Arise from slumber, my Beloved Friends! Shake free from the apathy and cheap pleasures of the world and raise a standard! Righteousness and justice our banners, with the drumbeat of love moving us forward, unified, 'til all our enemies are brought low! Every mountain, a smooth plain!

My God who has promised is faithful to do it!

# CLAMOR

*Let all bitterness, wrath, anger, clamor, and slander be put away*
*from you along with all malice. Be kind to one another...*
*– EPHESIANS 4:31–32*

Ilooked up the word "clamor" in *Webster's New Universal Unabridged Dictionary* and found "popular outcry" as an explanation of the word.

It leads me to think of the popular themes in advertising media today. A few examples...take your vitamins, exercise, lower your fat intake, invest, get a college degree, and on and on.

Are ANY of these popular themes in Scripture?

Perhaps we should humble ourselves and ask Father to please "Give us this day our daily bread." We should "Wait upon the Lord, and renew our strength," and "Give and it shall be given to us." How far we have fallen from His will and from His ways!

Let's get back to God's Word to us before we are swallowed up by the popular outcry. Although these messages may have good advice, let us never forget that our God is a faithful, intimate Father to us. He desires for us to depend on Him as children depend on their parents.

*Let all bitterness, wrath, anger, clamor, and evil speaking*
*be put away from you, with all malice. And be kind to one*
*another, tenderhearted, forgiving one another,*
*even as God in Christ forgave you.*
*– EPHESIANS 4:31–32*

# THE WHITE HORSE

As I was resting in the Lord, I saw Him seated upon a white horse. The part that was most clear was the horse's chest, flanks, and his tossing head. He was muscular and straining, his feet pawing at the ground, tension in every joint and sinew building to be released.

Even His horse is eager to come!

Crowned with anthems
Awaiting the date
The Father has set
He will not be late

His horse, restrained
Chomps at the plate
Restless for release
To plow through the gate

Behold Him! Come!
The KING OF KINGS!
Seated in splendor
Victory He brings!

Glory!

*Now I saw heaven opened, and behold, a white horse.*
*And He who sat on him was called Faithful and True,*
*and in righteousness He judges and makes war.*
*– REVELATION 19:11*

# They Roared in Vain

Oh! These mingled tears
Which pour
Sustained by Thy dear love

River roaring
Life outpouring

Mingled cup of blood
Which poured
Bulls of Bashan
Oh! How they roared!

*Many bulls have surrounded Me;*
*Strong bulls of Bashan have encircled Me.*
*– Psalm 22:12*

*So when Jesus had received the sour wine, He said, "It is finished!"*
*And bowing His head, He gave up His spirit.*
*– John 19:30*

# PURPLE

Blended with Him, one
Now two
United to put on one new shoe
Hers a pink
His a blue
Both put off
For one new shoe

Walking a lifetime path
As one
Bearing burdens
Having fun
Looking behind where we have trod
Leaving the fingerprints of God
Here a daughter
There a son
Look what Father hath begun

What a glorious path we've made
Turning heart clods with His spade
Walking along this path with God
Seeing royalty where once we trod

Hers a pink
And his a blue
Mingled now in one new shoe

*Therefore a man shall leave his father and mother and be joined*
*to his wife, and they shall become one flesh.*
*– Genesis 2:24*

# JUST BELIEVE

O ur pastor taught from Luke 8:40–56 on Sunday, and my mind took a different track from the one he took. The Holy Spirit does that as the Word is broken and multiplied—here a piece and there a piece, dishing out to each as we need a different insight.

In the recorded account, the synagogue leader, Jairus, came seeking Jesus, desperate for a miracle for his dying twelve-year-old daughter. What? A leader of the synagogue seeking Jesus?! Didn't the leaders of the synagogue become furious with Jesus early in His public ministry (Lk 21:28–30)? They drove Him out and wanted to stone Him. What was Jairus thinking! He could soon be out of a job and kicked out of the synagogue. He was putting his safety and reputation on the line, and everyone was watching.

However, in spite of the crowd, Jairus falls at Jesus' feet, pleading. He had reached a place of desperation far beyond the importance of job, reputation, or pride. But Jesus is pursuing an even deeper work in him.

Then, before Jesus could get away from the crowd to go with Jairus, some men came and reported that his daughter had died. Perhaps they were some of his good friends, people who cared a great deal for him and his family. Did they want to spare him sorrow upon sorrow by interrupting this flow of events that would surely jeopardize his reputation or even ruin it beyond repair? What could he possibly gain, seeking out this Jesus, when his daughter was dead? Surely, even worse would come of it.

Jesus sensed Jairus' fear. "Don't be afraid, just believe and she will be healed." His words refocused Jairus back to the faith that first brought him to Jesus. Just believe.

There was a long walk back to the house with many eyes watching and ridiculing words hissing through the air. The wailing of family, friends, and even professional mourners could be heard from a distance.

When Jesus, Jairus, and the rest of the crowd arrived on the scene, Jesus was very sure of Himself. It's as if He had thrown a handful of gunpowder into the frenzied moment by declaring, "She is not dead, but asleep." Scornful laughter exploded. In a state of extreme mental anguish, Jairus saw Jesus, calm and confident. His words rang in Jairus' heart, "Just believe."

Jesus put everyone out of the house, inviting only the little girl's parents and His inner trio of friends, Peter, James, and John. The grief-stricken, bewildered parents are hanging on to belief by a fragile thread.

What happened next was pure God! Taking her by the hand, He said, "Little one, get up." Her spirit returned from wherever it was lingering, and she got up! Astonishment? You bet! Jairus's belief exploded! Now he KNEW this Jesus was the One to believe in spite of his own reputation and beyond all doubt.


Hmmmm....

Is there something about coming to Him, stripped of reputation, vulnerable, naked, and empty?


About our closest friends and those who love us
best having good answers, true, but…


Just believe


The RIGHT answer has been given—Jesus Lord of All!
Forsaking all and clinging to Him
Hearing His Word and wavering not


That One who came into your heart

When deep despair became my lord
God meant it only
For my good
Upon my tear-stained
Cuff and sleeve
God whispered softly
Just believe

*But when Jesus heard it, He answered him, saying,*
*"Do not be afraid; only believe, and she will be made well."*
*– Luke 8:50*

# HE LONGS TO LOVE

*"O Jerusalem, Jerusalem, the one who kills the prophets and*
*stones those who are sent to her! How often I wanted to gather*
*your children together, as a hen gathers her chicks under her*
*wings, but you were not willing!"*
*– MATHEW 23:37*

We are not made so that we can love God. Not primarily. Rather, we
are created that God might love us. The outpouring of His love for
us stretches us, creating vessels that are fillable.

From His perspective the capacity to fill is limitless. From my per-
spective, the capacity to be filled is quite restricted. He keeps working to
expand my capacity and ability to be fully loved by Him.

God our Father is always, always, always yearning and looking for
ways to bless and love His children.

For remember...

*Every good gift and every perfect gift is from above,*
*and comes down from the Father of lights, with whom*
*there is no variation or shadow of turning.*
*– JAMES 1:17*

*We love Him because He first loved us.*
*– 1 JOHN 4:19*

# Grace Bends
# the Back

Oh how wrong I've been
I saw a bride without wrinkle or spot
Standing straight and elegantly attired
In robes of linen and garments of silk

He sees a servant
Suffering and hot
With a cloak of weariness
Upon his back

To the world belongs the walk of elegance

Regal status
Lifted head
Spotless gown
Full of dread
Dread of future, fear of man
Careful to stick to the whole plan
Watch your step
You might fall
Careful
Full of care
Careful now

Ah, the freedom to be bent
Bent within the Master's tent
Bent and sullied

Spent somehow
All for the want
To hear His call

Perseverance in weariness is grace

Grace not lack
Bends the back
And causes the walk to be different
Appealing

He seeks a partner
Bowed and broken
Soiled in service
Bathed in Grace

How wrong I've been
For my focus was
On me
Not Him

*But He gives more grace. Therefore He says:*
*"God resists the proud, but gives grace to the humble."*
*– JAMES 4:6*

*Humble yourselves in the sight of the Lord,*
*and He will lift you up.*
*– JAMES 4:10*

# Dressed Only in Scars

*In the evening she went, and in the morning she returned to the*
*second house of the women, to the custody of Shaashgaz, the king's*
*eunuch who kept the concubines. She would not go in to the king*
*again unless the king delighted in her and called for her by name.*
*Now when the turn came for Esther the daughter of Abihail the*
*uncle of Mordecai, who had taken her as his daughter, to go in to*
*the king, she requested nothing but what Hegai the king's eunuch,*
*the custodian of the women, advised. And Esther obtained favor*
*in the sight of all who saw her.*

*– Esther 2:14–15*

You summon me by name
I come before You with nothing
Clothed only in the scars of
Your love

# ROOM FOR DISTRACTION

I remember when my son had his first vision exam at age six. There was way too much yardage for his imagination to run wild between him and the big "E." It was a big flop.

Your Word, O Lord, is a lamp to my feet and a light to my path. I look closely and see my next step. I look up and I see the light to which I am headed. Let me not get caught up or stuck in the clamor, activity, and vanity in the distance between the foot lamp and the Light!

> *Your word is a lamp to my feet*
> *And a light to my path.*
>
> – PSALM 119:105

# URGENCY

It is nigh thee, even at the door!
Listen to the urgency of that message. If we would only believe. How clear the Father is in His message to us. The Sprit comes knocking. So near! Much, even all, can be changed in such a small second, everything as we know it changed in an instant of time. All our going forward can change direction in one breath of God.

Ages ago I saw with utter clarity a sudden change of direction that put a totally new set of circumstances before me and changed me for all time.

We are living in such an age. He is nigh thee, even at the door.

*So you also, when you see these things happening,*
*know that it is near—at the doors!*

– MARK 13:29

# SWEET SURRENDER

Today there are so many distractions. Having walked with the Lord for many years, I still have to make decisions to avoid the endless clamor of the world, to say no to many good things, even those that would benefit me in some way.

For example, many times I have had to make the conscious decision to listen only to my husband. He is the head of our growing family, and many, many decisions ultimately rest on his shoulders. That means when he has made a decision I do not need to go on trying to convince him otherwise. It is time to move on.

It is increasingly important to listen and submit to the Lord and His refined instruction and not try to "convince Him otherwise" when He says something. He is honing a more inerrant life before me and I want to walk in it. It is not unfamiliar, for He is leading. Yet it is demanding, for old habits are not working in this new land.

Again, choosing what was okay and good yesterday could be very wrong today. He is leading me into a deeper dependence upon Him than I've ever known before.

Submitted to His perfection and utterly dependent on His perfect grace within me, I wonder about the next step. At the same time, I am filled with the wonder of His ways.

I feel His perfecting process.
He is a refiner's fire.

*But who can endure the day of His coming?*
*And who can stand when He appears?*
*For He is like a refiner's fire*
*And like launderers' soap.*
*– MALACHI 3:2*

# Draw Me

Open the gates of eternity
My soul's richest Hope
Send on wings of eagles
The answer to my cry

Draw me!
I will run after Thee!
My soul follows hard
After Thee

My richest Love
My deepest Hope
Holy! Holy! Holy!

*Draw me away!*
*We will run after you.*
*The king has brought me into his chambers.*
*We will be glad and rejoice in you.*
*We will remember your love more than wine.*
*Rightly do they love you.*

– Song of Solomon 1:4

# HEAVEN KNOWS

How large and far-reaching the prophets of old lived for God. I am amazed at the dedicated lives they lived and the great works they did for God and Israel.

My mind wanders to my own life and how small and narrow I live for Him. Yet He celebrates me, and all of heaven knows it! Just how can that be?! Such reason to pause—Selah.

Over round about me
Heaven's portal opens
Grace and mercy flow like rivers
Washing, drenching, soaking
Opening eyes to see opportunity
Opening mouths to shout victory
There before me, Jesus!
There rides victory
Pause. Sigh. Selah.

*The LORD your God in your midst,*
*The Mighty One, will save;*
*He will rejoice over you with gladness,*
*He will quiet you with His love,*
*He will rejoice over you with singing."*
– ZEPHANIAH 3:17

# LOVE

Agape love. The *New Bible Dictionary* defines "agape love" in Greek as "that highest and noblest form of love which sees something infinitely precious in its object." I love that!

Bishop Stephan Neill defined love as "a steady direction of the will towards another's lasting good."

Because of the infinite, unfathomable love Jesus had for the Father and for us, He set His mind to go up to Jerusalem. He knew He would be mocked, beaten, scourged, and crucified. He did it because He saw something in us that was precious beyond expression. He made a decision of His will, knowing the end result was for our eternal good.

This, indeed, is wondrous love!

*Now Jesus, going up to Jerusalem, took the twelve disciples*
*aside on the road and said to them, "Behold, we are going up to*
*Jerusalem, and the Son of Man will be betrayed to the chief priests*
*and to the scribes; and they will condemn Him to death, and*
*deliver Him to the Gentiles to mock and to scourge and to crucify.*
*And the third day He will rise again."*
*– MATTHEW 20:17–19*

# A Little Thing to Do

Oh Lord!
Give me something small and hidden
Some little thing to do
The great things I can't handle
They are way too much for me
My mind and heart are overcome
With all that's here to know
Just give me something small and hidden
Some little thing to do

*LORD, my heart is not haughty,*
*Nor my eyes lofty.*
*Neither do I concern myself with great matters,*
*Nor with things too profound for me.*
*– PSALM 131:1*

*And whatever you do in word or deed, do all in the name of the*
*Lord Jesus, giving thanks to God the Father through Him.*
*– COLOSSIANS 3:17*

# To My Beloved
# A Love Poem

How does one begin
To tell of One so rare
As Him
Of One so rare?

How does one place
A word upon a page
To describe a God
Man?

There is none so fair
In all of human speech
As my Beloved
None so fair

Who can count the stars
That my Beloved
Made for me?

Who can name them
One by one
As He?

Who can see into the deep
The creatures
He has made

Only He can see and
Laugh at their ungainly thrones.
Only He

Oh! There is only
One so fair
As my Beloved
Only one as He

*He counts the number of the stars;*
*He calls them all by name.*
– PSALM 147:4

# MY SCHEDULE HIS OWN

My Friday schedule cancelled until it was empty. I had a day set aside by the Lord, so I drew close to Him. He is so wonderful, so close in every way. He comes and my heart is moved with love; inexpressible, yet purely and simply expressed too. He never tires of my simple attempts. He is never offended if I break protocol. When He is dressed in glory I may still run to Him with joy and laughter and reckless abandon, that freedom known only between children and someone they wholly trust.

He comes with such a glorious gift every time. I am always undone in tears and thankfulness.

> How can it be so my Love
> How do you suppose
> You take a child such as me
> And frame me like a rose
>
> How can You regard a one
> So small and helpless, so impure
> You set upon a Rock my feet
> And make my walk secure
>
> You have an eye upon Your child
> My heart leaps with joy untold
> The Father made one such as me
> To be among His fold
>
> And now You gather in Your arms
> This young one and her kin

To make of them one new formed bride
A special one for Him

Your Son will see this gathered tribe
Our arms raised high as one
To receive His gift so full and free
The Father's Only Son!

Oh, Come our Savior! Come our King!
Oh, Come Thou Mighty Prince!
Your Bride from slumber does awake
Oh Come! Oh Come! Make haste!

*And the Spirit and the bride say, "Come!" And let him who hears
say, "Come!" And let him who thirsts come. Whoever desires,
let him take the water of life freely.*
*– REVELATION 22:17*

# Pillars of Light

We the Bride would be Your walking pillars of light and love on the earth. Let no darkness of fear come in our way. Let the cries of evil remain outside the city gate. Let no soul within be frightened. Let wise counsel rise among the humble of heart and bring true Sabbath rest upon Your anointed.

Mighty Lion of Judah come to earth
Announced Your presence
From Your berth
Holy Ones upon us blow
Enemies scattered with Your roar
Saints and angels bow below

Breath of Lion strong
Fill us now
With Spirit song

Set our feet upon the Rock
Though all else fail
You will not be mocked

Holy One, Mighty, Strong,
Judge now the world for it's wrong
Let the night grow blacker still
Until its darkness be fulfilled

Birth the dawning ore Your Bride
Bright like that of moonlit sky

Center ore her with Thy robe
'Til all nations bow as one
Giving to the Royal Son
All the honor power praise

Glorious Father
Begotten Son
Spirit sent
Make us one

*The LORD also will roar from Zion,*
*And utter His voice from Jerusalem;*
*The heavens and earth will shake;*
*But the LORD will be a shelter for His people,*
*And the strength of the children of Israel.*
*– JOEL 3:16*

*And the Spirit and the bride say, "Come!"*
*And let him who hears say, "Come!"*
*– REVELATION 22:17*

# My Weakness
# His Opportunity

This ever-growing weakness in my body, as I rest day after day trying to heal, is causing diminishing muscle strength and stamina, less than I've ever experienced before. I depend on the sure promises of the Lord's New and Living Covenant to strengthen me for every need.

As I live daily to do His will, His strength in me will be there to make that service to Him most glorious. I am not so concerned about my weakness. The service *to* Jesus is so different from the service *for* Jesus.

The seasons of service for Jesus were so good. It was, and still is, hard to let go of that precious time of doing.

The time of service to Jesus has arrived. It is most sweet and altogether desirable and superior to previous times.

Jesus has taught me how to sing to Him. I lift my voice in melodies old and new every day, and He is most pleased. He walks with me, sups with me, sits with me, teaches—oh, how He teaches! He causes me to be still in His arms.

This season of service to Jesus, allowing Him, receiving Him, welcoming His service to me is a very humbling time. It is a big paradigm shift for me.

Previously, God's love displayed itself by correcting me. Over the years, I grew to easily take and eagerly receive His correction and conviction. This is so very different. Oh, this is so very, very different! It is friendship full and free.

Over and over each day, I began to ask Holy Spirit (My Best Help) to expand my capacity to receive Father's love, to break me forth on every side, stretching me and stretching me. Each day I was ready for more stretching. For weeks I prayed, "Oh, expand my capacity to receive Your love, Papa! Stretch me more! I long to know who You are, Lord! I long to receive You! I just *must* know You! I must have You!"

> *Enlarge the place of your tent,*
> *And let them stretch out the curtains of your dwellings;*
> *Do not spare; lengthen your cords,*
> *And strengthen your stakes.*
> *– ISAIAH 54:2*

And I think, in His own dear gentle way, He is. He is teaching me more deeply about the cross. Now I can wholeheartedly cry with the Apostle Paul, "I will not glory save in the cross of my Lord Jesus Christ!" (Galatians 6:14a)

With songs of joy, I embrace my cross and follow! Oh, my yes! What an exchange! My life for His?? My will for His!? Oh, please, please, please! The New Covenant in His Blood, who can grasp that? There is so much love poured out in it I am only just beginning, at the very brink, of the knowledge of His Mighty Depths.

And now, the latter rain is here! The Holy Spirit has stretched and stretched at Father's bidding and has begun to pour.

> *Be glad then, you children of Zion,*
> *And rejoice in the LORD your God;*
> *For He has given you the former rain faithfully,*
> *And He will cause the rain to come down for you—*

> *The former rain,*
> *And the latter rain in the first month.*
> *– JOEL 2:23*

There is a new song in my heart, wonderful, filled with wonder, open and clean. It feels like the paradigm shifted right through me.

I am on the other side, still getting my bearings, alive,
watchful, expectant.

Daily I see such goodness and love in so many areas of my life.
Today I am able not only to see it and be thankful, but also to
embrace and rejoice over it. For I know it is Father's love
being poured into me.

Though I may never again have the strength to dance for Him,
I have a song for my Beloved that He Himself sings through me.
Father listens and is so pleased.

Latter rain!
Latter rain!
Let it rain!
The Spirit and the Bride say, "Come!"

*The threshing floors shall be full of wheat,*
*And the vats shall overflow with new wine and oil.*
– *JOEL 2:24*

# TENDER CRACKING

My soul crumbles with thanksgiving to the Lord for all the many things He has done for me. I cannot even lift my head. My tears pour into His hands. Daily He leads me with benefits and at night He restores my strength, preparing a new seamless path for me to walk. He is so gentle and good.

My heart needs His gentleness today. I need what He alone has for me and I hide in the shelter of His cupped nail-scarred hands, feeling like a small seed awaiting burial.

What a good place to die, in the hands of the very best lover known to man. He surely knows how and when to plant, He knows when to set the seed upon the shelf to await planting. He knows when conditions are right to take that seed down and tenderly crack its thick shell and soak it in tears. He alone knows the harvest it will bring.

Oh, Holy Spirit!
Help me do my best
In humble service
In Sabbath rest
Letting faith be my guide
Never for myself alone
For others
Keep me going home

*Most assuredly, I say to you, unless a grain of wheat*
*falls into the ground and dies, it remains alone;*
*but if it dies, it produces much grain.*
*– JOHN 12:24*

# Holy Dread

The account of Ananias and Sapphira in Acts Chapter 5, and the holy dread that came upon the church because of the judgment of God, really hit me today. I know I am prone to the same sin they fell under. They wanted to look good to their leaders. Guilty! They were greedy. Guilty! They promoted themselves as something better than they were. Guilty! They treated lightly the needs of the body of Christ. Guilty! They didn't esteem God and take Him seriously. Guilty! I don't have the holy reverence for Him that He deserves.

Thank You, Jesus, in that while I was yet a sinner, You chose to lay down Your life for me. Yes, You took the cross that was rightfully mine to bear, so that I could go free!

Oh, thank You my Lord!
Oh, thank You my Love!
Your life-saving, life-giving blood
Covers me!
Hid from sin's dreadful curse I stand,
Cleared and righteous in my Father's hand!
Redeemed!
Set free to hate the sin!
Set free to love and adore my King!

Oh, I am so thankful!

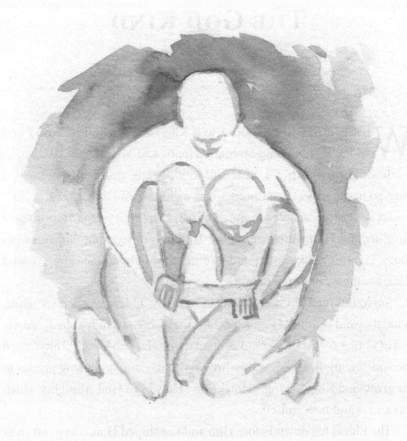

*Seeing then that we have a great High Priest who has passed
through the heavens, Jesus the Son of God, let us hold fast our
confession. For we do not have a High Priest who cannot sympa-
thize with our weaknesses, but was in all points tempted as we
are, yet without sin. Let us therefore come boldly to the
throne of grace, that we may obtain mercy and find grace
to help in time of need.*
– HEBREWS 4:14–16

# ROYALTY –
# THE GOD KIND

What is it like to be subject to a King? A King full of Power and Glory, Wisdom and Strength, Honor and Might?

Jesus is such a friend, near and kind, gentle and dearly beloved! I must go to the pages of Scripture to get a glimpse of His Majesty.

In Revelation chapter 4, much of it is displayed in the responses of those around Him. Father upon the Throne is unseen but violent in His Glory. Lightnings like jasper and sardine stone light up the skies. Around Him, a rainbow like an emerald.

Surrounding Him were four and twenty Elders clothed in white. What they did signifies High Kingship. They were carefully robed, orderly seated until it seems they could contain themselves no longer. They joined the Four Living Beasts near the throne who day and night sing praises to the great God King, saying, "Holy! Holy! Holy Lord God Almighty which was and is and is to come!"

The Elders fell down before Him and worshiped Him. They cast their crowns at His feet and added their own song to the song of the beasts, saying, "Thou art worthy, Oh Lord, to receive glory and honor and power for Thou has created all things and for Thy pleasure they are and were created."

Kingship!
Violent and demanding
In its splendor!
Before it,
who can stand?

*Therefore God also has highly exalted Him and given Him the name which is above every name, that at the name of Jesus every knee should bow, of those in heaven, and of those on earth, and of those under the earth, and that every tongue should confess that Jesus Christ is Lord, to the glory of God the Father.*

– PHILIPPIANS 2:9–11

# Dying Is Not Loss

Joel 2:21. "Fear not O land, be glad and rejoice for the Lord has done great things!"

Vs. 23. "Be glad then you children of Zion and rejoice in the Lord your God! For He gives you the former rains in just measure and in righteousness and He causes the former rain and the latter rain as before."

Vs. 27. "And my people shall never be put to shame...."

Vs. 28. "And afterward, I will pour out my Spirit upon all (ALL) flesh...." (Amplified Bible)

Father is so bold to give such wonderfully good news in the midst of affliction! He fills my heart with tears and laughter at the same time. I weep for His goodness to me. I weep for those in the Valley of Decision. His goodness is near to them, too. They just need to call to Him for help and He will be there. In His divine majesty and sovereign love He calls to them. All who hear and answer will be called His People. Amazing King!

Wherever did You come from
Thou great and terrible King
The likes of You has not been known
Since past remembering

The Way that You established
When You died upon the cross

Gave us a keen example
That to die was not a loss

How odd You are, my darling King
To lay down Your life and die
That I a one so sin-composed
Might on Your Way rely
And bear my own cross
Eagerly
For dying is not loss

# LET NOTHING TERRIFY

1 Peter 3:6 – "It was thus that Sarah obeyed Abraham (following his guidance and leadership over her by) calling him Lord, Master, leader, authority. And you are now her true daughters if you do right and let nothing terrify you – not giving way to hysterical fears or letting anxieties unnerve you." (Amplified Bible)

Ps. 68:11 – "The Lord gives the word [of power]: the women who bear and publish (the news) are a great host." (Amplified Bible)

Enough said!

# PIERCED THOUGH

The spear was thrust and
Cleaved the mountain
Of Your heart of
Holy love

Out flowed rivers of Living Water
Drenching
Washing
Making me whole

Free at last
To tremble on bended knee

Free at last to kiss
The face of the One
Who died
For me

*But one of the soldiers pierced His side with a spear, and*
*immediately blood and water came out.*
*– JOHN 19:34*

157

# WALLPAPER

How lovely become the interiors when Christ does the decorating. Several years ago, I took a therapeutic art class I really enjoyed. Among many other things we did, we made and decorated masks. One of the masks I decorated still speaks to me today.

Most of the folks taking the class decorated only the exterior of their plaster forms. I thought I must do the inside also as I had just recently had an interior mental breakthrough. Previously overwhelmed by it, I was once again able to plan, prepare, and enjoy a meal for my family. This was no small task as when they were all together our number had reached twenty-two.

I glued recipes into the interior of the mask, covering its insides. I added a simple brown button in the form of a heart, the only embellishment, out of love and humility.

As I think about God's promise to write His very Word on our hearts and in our minds, I am so deeply, unspeakably, humbled and thankful. Every small Word the Holy Spirit preaches is a blessing.

Oh, how He writes Himself on the inside of my skin and wallpapers His Word into my heart!

*But this is the covenant that I will make with the house of Israel*
*after those days, says the LORD: I will put My law in their minds,*
*and write it on their hearts; and I will be their God,*
*and they shall be My people.*

– JEREMIAH 31:33

# ANCIENT SONG FOREVER NEW

Every breath drawn
A great hush
The Gates swing open
Through it strides
The One the Only
The King of Eternity's Door
The Great and Mighty
I AM
The Shepherd King
A MAN

And every breath explodes in relief
He is for us
He is FOR US!
We are His and the sheep
Of His pasture
We reign as one
The Shepherd King
With Him
The Great I AM
We sing

The Mighty All-Consuming
King
Strides o'er the earth
The lost to bring
Into the shelter
Of His arms

Breathe peace, dear Bride
Over His lambs
Find them, weary lost cold numb
Breath of God
Upon them come
Another lamb unto Him calls
Open the door to the Glory Halls

Fathers face beams over all
Begins to sing
And silence falls
Nothing more can now
Be done
Only IN Jesus
Can we hear
This one

Ancient song forever new
Sung above below and through
Endless mercy full of grace
Gaze now upon your
Savior's face

*The LORD your God in your midst,*
*The Mighty One, will save;*
*He will rejoice over you with gladness,*
*He will quiet you with His love,*
*He will rejoice over you with singing.*
*– ZEPHANIAH 3:17*

# ABOUT THE AUTHOR

Jo Gwost is the wife of one, the mother of six, the grandmother of twelve. Though this is her first attempt at writing a book, she has been journaling for most of her married life. She learned about Jesus as a little girl and grew steadily towards accepting him as Savior and Lord. She lives with her husband, Jim, in St. Cloud Minnesota.

# ACKNOWLEDGMENTS

Special thanks to all the friends who believed I should.
For Kathy who believed I could,
Phillip who got it off the ground,
Emily and her tender microscopic view,
Jim who never stopped,
Also, Lyndon and his professional work,
Briana and hers,
And over all the Father who bought it all
about in His Grace and Mercy

# ILLUSTRATOR BIO

Illustrator Briana Ladwig loves storytelling with watercolor and pen.
She lives with her family in Wichita, Kansas.

www.ingramcontent.com/pod-product-compliance
Ingram Content Group UK Ltd.
Pitfield, Milton Keynes, MK11 3LW, UK
UKHW041723130325
456141UK00007B/90